Freedom Bargains

REV DR JOSHUA BOATENG

ISBN - 10: 1912420090
ISBN-13: 978-1912420094

DEDICATION

This book is dedicated to all the men and women who have impacted my Christian walk through their ministry, spiritual walk and dedication and their personal life example.

CONTENTS

ACKNOWLEDGMENTS

I am grateful to my wife Emelia, daughter Princella and sons Leroy and Jason, for enduring my many long nights on the computer. Big thank you to Rev Peter Vincent under whose ministry the sermon series from who this book arises was birthed. I am also grateful to Dr Ola Epemolu for always being a friend that sticks closer than a brother. Your reward will be great and your crowns many. Final thanks to all my other colleagues and partners in ministry who labour quietly and effectively in God's vineyard. Your labour will never be in vain.

Endorsements

In his latest offering, Rev Dr Joshua Boateng has shown how we can compromise our freedom by dangerous baits disguised as bargains. The apparent bargains are the bargains of commitment, compromise, community and cash! His central theme is that appealing and seemingly legitimate 'offers' and sinful situations are not friends to be toyed or played with, especially when presented as bargains! Dr Boateng proceeds to warn us about how sins and sinful situations are often presented to us as friends rather than the enemies that they are. The book is very readable and the issues that are dealt with transcends the Church into the community and society in general. It cuts across the racial, social status or educational divide. Freedom Bargains is highly recommended to everyone who wants to live in absolute freedom!

Rev Dr Ola Epemolu
Associate Pastor, Glasgow City Church. (Glasgow, UK)

Many people and even nations profess to be free and yet their realities on the ground do not match their expectations. Most nations for example have political independence and yet are economically dependent on others. Individuals seemingly have freedom of credit living and yet find themselves in bondage to debt. Some people, including Christian believers, equate freedom to license and end up in mental, emotional and spiritual bondage. That is because we can all easily fall prey to the small print of supposed freedom bargains, which is not complete. God desires that we do not settle for less than He intended but rather that we walk according to knowledge. Self-centred and self-conscious living, rather than God-centred and God-conscious living still leads men into the devil's trap of living below their creative potential. With this profound quote, 'do not settle for counterfeit or half price measures, no matter how appealing, when there is a more glorious, complete, divine revelation and provision', the author presents exploration of possibilities beyond face value as the route to maximizing one's potential and living the victorious Christian life. In this book, the author takes the story of Moses' encounter with Pharaoh and brings to life powerful life lessons that will challenge and inspire you in all aspects of your life. It is a practical, inspiring, easily readable and intellectually engaging material. I strongly commend this recent provision from Dr (Rev) Boateng as essential reading for every believer.

Rev Dr Philip Debrah
(Resident Pastor, Shalom Sanctuary, Victory Bible Church International, Kumasi; Lecturer, School of Pharmacy, University of Ghana, Legon)

Foreword

This is a brilliant piece! An inspiring and challenging exposition by Rev Dr Joshua Boateng.

In this Book, he truthfully states that: **"There is the tendency for believers to play along to the dangerous trappings of evil and ignore the negative consequences that follow. It is the same as someone playing in the deep end of a swimming pool when the individual knows full well that he or she cannot swim."**

Most people claim to be free and yet end up living a life of bondage because they accept baits that look so attractive on the outside, but which end up biting and leaving us in disappointment. It is very easy, in the current dispensation to compromise our values and settle for what is expedient even if it's less than God intended. Joshua takes up a well-known story of the Israelites escape from the slavery of Egypt and draws out vital lessons for all who desire to lead a life of complete and total freedom. You will learn how to aspire to and walk in complete freedom as you avoid and reject subtle traps (referred to as Bargains) in various avenues of life. The principles are applicable for whatever estate of life you're in whether in marriage, ministry, study, and career or in leadership. 'Freedom Bargains', will inspire you to pursue a life of excellence and to always aim for God's best for your life.

Rev (Dr) Frank Opoku Amoako

(Founder, Senior Pastor - Destiny Life International Church, Virginia, USA)

Preface

Every human being desires to be free even when subjected to a life time of extreme oppression, which is all they might know and accept. God created humanity with the innate desire and capacity to live in liberty. However, this can be interpreted and expressed to various degrees or extremes, which makes us live below the optimum state of freedom which God intends for us. This is dependent on the type of choices we make, and therefore places an element of responsibility upon us in terms of what we do with the promise of freedom which God has declared. This promise represents God's plans, intention and purpose for our lives as beautifully captured Jeremiah 29:11 as follows: "I know the plans I have for you, they are plans of good and not evil, to give you a future and a hope (bring you to an expected end)". Some people completely miss the opportunity for freedom by doing nothing, others experience snippets of it because they're only willing to go so far and therefore settle for less, whilst still others go all the way to experience all that God intends for them, which is complete freedom in Christ, even if it means delayed gratification. When Christ came to earth, He came for the purpose of restoring to God's original intention, but before then, God had already laid out His clear intention, all of which were illustrated to us through the journeys of the nation of Israel who experienced slavery in Egypt and subsequently led out to freedom by Moses, even though it will take them 40 years to eventually reach their desired destination. Of them Paul, wrote in the book of 1st Corinthians 10: 1-11. **"For I do not want you to be ignorant of the fact, brothers and sisters, that our ancestors were all under the cloud and that they all passed through the sea. They were all baptized into Moses in the cloud and in the sea. They all ate the same spiritual food and drank the same spiritual drink; for they drank from the spiritual rock that accompanied them, and that rock was Christ. Nevertheless, God was not pleased with most of them; ... These things happened to them as examples and were written down as warnings for us, on whom the culmination of the ages has come."** These examples of old are still relevant to us today, because though human civilization has progressed to unrecognisable levels compared to even centuries before, human nature has not changed much and therefore, there are always great lessons to learn from history. In this book, we will explore some of the pitfalls that could jeopardize our complete freedom in Christ but more importantly, learn the principles that will enable you to operate in the plans and purposes of God so you flourish in His perfect will and fulfil your full potential. I pray you will be blessed abundantly as you read and ponder over these principles.

1 FREE INDEED

"The truth you know will set you free. What you know you will believe, what you believe you become".

Bishop David Oyedepo

"... It was for freedom that Christ set us free, no longer to be subject to a yoke of slavery, so we're rejoicing, in God's victory, our hearts responding to His love".

John Gibson

The above chorus was one of the very first songs I learned when I first arrived in the United Kingdom. It is inspired by Galatians chapter 5 where Paul examines salvation through new life in Christ and not by the outward manifestations of religious activity. Portions of Galatians 5:1-16 are quoted below:

"It is for freedom that Christ has set us free. Stand firm, then, and do not let yourselves be burdened again by a yoke of slavery... You, my brothers and sisters, were called to be free. But do not use your freedom to indulge the flesh; rather, serve one another humbly in love. For the entire law is fulfilled in keeping this one command: "Love your neighbour as yourself." If you bite and devour each other, watch out or you will be destroyed by each other. So I say, walk by the Spirit, and you will not gratify the desires of the flesh".

Jesus Christ came to earth as a man, experienced all the frailties of humanity and yet was without sin. He ultimately conquered sin and death through His death, burial and resurrection (1 Corinthians 15) to purchase for us eternal life and not just that, but abundant life. During His life on earth, He said among other things that **"whoever the Son sets free is free indeed"**. Unfortunately, most of us settle for less, in the name of religiosity, false humility and traditions that **"makes the gospel of no effect"**.

1

The best part of this book is about Moses' encounter with Pharaoh as he pursued God's mission to deliver the children of Israel from slavery in Egypt and we will consider the discourse that ensued between Pharaoh and Moses. Chapters one to twelve of Exodus describe the Israelites in bondage, their cry for deliverance, Moses' encounter with God, his commissioning to lead them out of slavery and the events leading to their final liberation. The question, is what was the purpose of their liberation? In our case as Christian believers, why did God send Jesus to secure our salvation? In what areas of our lives do we need to experience complete freedom in order to serve and worship God as He promised in His word? The following portions of scripture paint a lovely picture of God's divine purpose in saving us and how he wants us to live and function after we have experienced this awesome salvation: Exodus 7:16; Exodus 8:1; Ephesians 2:8-10 and 1 Peter 2:9-11.

"Then the LORD said to Moses, "Pharaoh's heart is unyielding; he refuses to let the people go. Go to Pharaoh in the morning as he goes out to the river. Confront him on the bank of the Nile, and take in your hand the staff that was changed into a snake. Then say to him, 'The LORD, the God of the Hebrews, has sent me to say to you: **Let my people go, so that they may worship me in the wilderness**. But until now you have not listened".

Exodus 7:14-16

"Then the LORD said to Moses, "Go to Pharaoh and say to him, **'this is what the LORD says: Let my people go, so that they may worship me**".

Exodus 8:1

"For it is by grace you have been saved, through faith - and this is not from yourselves, it is the gift of God - not by works, so that no one can boast. **For we are God's handiwork (masterpiece), created in Christ Jesus to do good works, which God prepared in advance for us to do**".

Ephesians 2: 8-10

"But you are a chosen people, a royal priesthood, a holy nation, God's special possession, **that you may declare the praises of him who called you out of darkness into his wonderful light**".

1 Peter 2: 9

It is very easy to lose our priorities, sense of purpose and vision, which is why Solomon said "**where there is no vision, the people perish or cast off restraint**". In other words, we can compromise our values and settle for what is expedient even if it's less than God intended. As a result, anything goes as long as it does not appear sinful and satisfies our conscience. The above verses are three wonderful scriptures of immense proportions and enormous spiritual implications. They reveal God's intended level of spirituality as Adam enjoyed in the "cool of the morning", and Moses experienced, when he saw God face to face for 40 days. The shocking truth is we're happy to settle for less.

According to Exodus 7 verse16, the children of Israel were delivered from Egypt (the land of slavery and bondage), in order to worship God. This was a very specific pronouncement which we will explore in more detail in the subsequent chapters. This instruction has always been under assault, and even Jesus Christ Himself experienced this assault when He was tempted by Satan.

In Ephesians chapter 2, Paul continues his amazing discussion about the spiritual blessings which every believer enjoys in Christ beginning from Ephesians 1 verse 4. In chapter 2, he compares where God picked us from, our new privileged position and new life in Christ, how He achieved this, our new condition and His purpose for saving us. Adam, the first man sinned by disobeying, though God had warned him about the consequences of his sin (**Genesis 2 verses 15-17**). These consequences were:

> Spiritual death – separation from God, the source of life
> Physical death – separation of soul from the body
> Eternal death – eternal separation of body and soul from God

What did Christ do? (Ephesians 2 verses 1-6)
Jesus went to the ultimate depth by being born as a man; He experienced every temptation and human pain including sickness; He

3

was crucified, died, buried and raised to life again. However, in the process, he raised us to the ultimate heights as summarised below:

He made us alive w**ith Christ** – Our New Condition (Ephesians 2:5)
He raised us up **with Christ** – Our New Dimension (Ephesians 2:6a)
He seated us up **with Christ** – Our New Position (Ephesians 2:6b)

Each of the above 3 conditions in Ephesians 2 verses 5 - 6 conveys a truth regarding our salvation. Not only are we together with Christ, but we are so united and identified together with Him that no one can separate us from Him or Him from us. Only we can choose to turn our backs on Him. Do you realise the enormity of this divine transition? It is the same people, without hope and destined for the slaughter house as described in Ephesians 2 verses 1 – 3, who enjoy this triple transformation. This was all done through Christ and all of it on his account not our own works. Though we deserved death as a result of sin, God, did not give us what we deserved (death) because of His grace and mercy, but rather gave us what we did not deserve, (i.e. new life). Most men try to decorate religion, church tradition, guilty conscience, false humility, charity and good works as salvation but that is a losing battle. In the bible, a donkey was also referred to as an ass and reminds me of the saying that "a **decorated donkey is still an ass**". Here is the point, "**people are not sinners because they sin; they sin because they are sinners**". Christ did not come to embalm humanity to make preserved mummies out of us. Rather, He died and rose again to give us resurrection life and flight to glorified life in the heavenly places in Christ. Please read the whole of Ephesians to get the full picture of this exciting prospect.

The question then is whether Christ can be bound by sins and transgression and the answer is a definite no. He is alive and not dead in sins and transgression, **so are you**. He's resurrected and not buried, **so are you** and he's seated above and not beneath, **so are you**. Unfortunately Christians tend to live like Lazarus when he came out of the grave. We live and function below our new potential because though we've been given new life, we still hold on to our grave clothes. Ephesians chapter 2 verse 10 says "**we are his workmanship (masterpiece), created (or recreated) in Christ Jesus unto good works**". He's done the work of salvation and paid the price but that is so we can live out good works. We should remove the grave clothes and enter into newness of life as children of the king, seated in heavenly places, because although we are in the world, we are not of this world. That is why the Holy Spirit was given (Romans 8 verse11). The bottom line is that:

What Christ is we are   – Alive
What Christ has we have   – New Life
Where Christ is we are   – Heavenly Places

This leads us nicely into the third scripture from 1 Peter 2 verse 9, which captures beautifully what we are and not what we are trying to be. First of all we are chosen, (one of the 7 spiritual blessings listed in Ephesians chapter 1). Secondly, we are to be priests of the 'Great High Priest' and kings of the 'King of kings'. Priests and kings had well defined functions of teaching the law and being in government respectively. Thirdly, we are described as a holy nation, people who share in God's divine nature. All these three levels of calling were for the purpose of being God's representatives on earth, showing forth His praises on the earth so that everyone will know there is a living God.

Therefore the title to this chapter is true. The person whom Jesus sets free, is "free indeed" to live life on a higher plane, to function with God's authority and to have abundant life as Jesus Christ promised. Do we believe it strongly enough to live it and eventually manifest the things God says we are? Well the devil and his agents believe it, but they cannot become that and so they will do all in their power, to rob you of your inheritance in Christ and from fulfilling God's purpose for keeping you on earth even for a few more weeks.

We must know and experience this truth, because "the truth we know we believe, and what we believe, we become", as noted by Bishop Oyedepo. Do you believe that Jesus Christ has paid it all? Do you want to walk and live in freedom? Then let's read on as we unpack and explore this subject in the ensuing chapters. Remember, he whom the Son shall set free is free indeed.

CHPATER 2 THE ENEMY IS NOT YOUR FRIEND

"The thief comes only to steal, to kill and destroy".
John 10:10a

The title of this chapter appears somewhat contradictory, however, it captures the tendency for believers to play along to the dangerous trappings of evil and ignoring the negative consequences that follow. It's no different from someone playing in the deep end of a swimming pool when the individual knows full well that he or she cannot swim. Most of us will have been told as kids, "never to speak to a stranger". Those of us who are parents will probably have done the same, not to be repressive but to protect our children.

It is disingenuous on the part of politicians, media commentators, journalists and certain sections of society, to disregard biblical principles that seek to protect us from acts and lifestyles that do more harm than good. In the same way that we seek to protect our children, we should never entertain the works of the devil who will even fake angelic attributes just to ensnare us. He always seeks someone to devour, but the problem is, he does not always show up the way you expect him to. The depiction of the devil in artworks and movies as an ugly monster, dressed in dark Halloween clothes is probably one of the greatest tricks ever played on the church and society in general. In several places within the bible, we are warned with phrases such as **'trickery of the devil'**, **'an angel of light'**, **'prowls around like a lion seeking someone to devour'**, **'give no place to the devil'** and **'resist the devil'**. So you see, the enemy will not always come against you in ways you expect, which is why we need to be alert.

For the sake of balance, it is important to mention that we sometimes blame too much on the devil, when in fact, we should take personal responsibility. For example, we should stop blaming the devil when we are tempted about overeating, browsing internet pornography, fornicating and committing adultery. The truth is that most of these sins arise because we feed the lust of our sinful nature which has nothing to do with the devil. All we need to do is stop and if you're struggling, seek help from a trusted friend to hold you accountable so that with prayer and the help of the Spirit, you will overcome it. The other extreme, which is also a great deception, is the belief that any mention of the devil is mere superstition. Jesus taught a lot about the devil, having personally encountered Him on several occasions during his ministry. The devil is described as the 'prince of the power of the air' and 'ruler of the kingdom of darkness'.

The bible is not clear about the source of evil, however, the first time sin (or rather iniquity) was mentioned, in the bible before creation of man, it appeared in the heart of the devil, who exalted himself in wanting to become like God. Whilst there is debate about who created evil, it is quite clear from Genesis chapter 1, that God did not create evil and the darkness. In fact, God's first act in the process of creating the heavens and the earth, was to create light to dispel the darkness and God specifically separated the light from the darkness (Genesis 1:3-4). It goes on to say that God saw everything He had made and it was good. Therefore, anything associated with the devil, cannot be our companion. According to the bible, the devil, through the serpent deceived Eve and caused Adam to sin (Genesis 3:1-13, Revelation 12:7-12), wreaking great havoc upon the human race, for which we suffer the consequences today.

The devil has always opposed God's plans and agenda. God has cast him away from heaven and judged him to eternal damnation, therefore, there's no way he can be your friend. He attacked and destroyed whole nations, families and individuals alike, including Job, Saul and Judas. He sought to "sift Peter as wheat", causing him to deny Christ, he attacked Paul's ministry on many fronts and he still does the same against the church today. You might say, well, I have never liked the devil, in fact I hate him, but there are only two absolutes as far as kingdom dynamics are concerned. Anytime we move outside God's will, we give ground to the devil and it is important that we repent and recover, so we don't grow dull and give him any more ground. Let us briefly explore two case studies, one at the very beginning of humanity and the other at the start of Jesus' earthly ministry.

Eve (Genesis chapter 3, verses 1-13)

"Now the serpent was more crafty than any other beast of the field that the LORD God had made. He said to the woman, did God actually say, you shall not eat of any tree in the garden'? And the woman said to the serpent, we may eat of the fruit of the trees in the garden, but God said, 'you shall not eat of the fruit of the tree that is in the midst of the garden, neither shall you touch it, lest you die. But the serpent said to the woman, you will not surely die. **For God knows that when you eat of it your eyes will be opened, and you will be like God, knowing good and evil**. So when the woman saw that the tree was good for food, and that it was a delight to the eyes, and that the tree was to be desired to make one wise, she took of its fruit and ate, and she also gave some to her husband who was with her, and he ate. Then the eyes of both were opened, and they knew that they were naked. And they sewed fig leaves together and made themselves loincloths. And they heard the sound of the LORD God walking in the garden in the cool of the day, and the man and his wife hid themselves from the presence of the LORD God among the trees of the garden. But the LORD God called to the man and said to him, where are you? And he said, I heard the sound of you in the garden, and I was afraid, because I was naked, and I hid myself. He said, who told you that you were naked? Have you eaten of the tree of which I commanded you not to eat? The man said, the woman whom you gave to be with me, she gave me fruit of the tree, and I ate. Then the LORD God said to the woman, what is this that you have done? The woman said, the serpent deceived me, and I ate."

(Genesis 3:1-13, ESV)

This short episode in the drama of human existence wreaked the greatest havoc upon the human race and upon everything that God created in perfect condition. If only Adam and Eve had known and remembered that the devil never had their interest at heart. There were 4 key misrepresentations, misconceptions and half-truths which the devil managed to sow into the mind of Eve, and thereby deceive her and Adam into disobeying God:

1. **"Has God actually said"** – He sought to dilute the seriousness of God's command to them as an absolute

instruction which they needed to obey. Half obedience is no obedience at all. It does not surprise me at all when institutions and individuals, question the importance of anything related to God.

2. **"You will be like God"** – This was definitely not the whole truth and caused a serious crisis of identity. This is because in Genesis chapter 1 verse 26-27, God Himself had taken the initiative to create humanity (male and female) in the image of God and given them a mandate to rule and look after the earth. In other words, they were God's representatives on earth and did not need any more make up to boost their identities.

It is important to carefully note, what the serpent said specifically in Genesis 3 verse 5 "For God knows that when you eat from it your eyes will be opened, and you will be like God, knowing good and evil." Interestingly, after God had confronted Adam, Eve and the serpent, God repeated part of this statement, which clearly shows how subtle the devil was in planting half-truths.

"Then the LORD God said, "Behold, the man has become like one of Us, to know good and evil. And now, lest he put out his hand and take also of the tree of life, and eat, and live forever" therefore the LORD God sent him out of the garden of Eden to till the ground from which he was taken. So He drove out the man; and He placed cherubim at the east of the Garden of Eden, and a flaming sword which turned every way, to guard the way to the tree of life."

Genesis 3:22 – 24

However, though it will appear God was agreeing with the serpent's assertion, a closer look at the two statements reveals clear distinctions. Firstly, the serpent said their eyes will be opened, but did not specify what their eyes would open to see. As Adam and Eve found out, to their own detriment, their eyes did not open to become like God, but rather opened to their own sinfulness, nakedness and limitations outside of God's will. Unfortunately, this led to feelings of shame as well as blaming each other and God. Secondly, I believe that God, in making that statement, acknowledges their exposure to the conflict between good and evil, but sadly, it was not to increased power and authority. They did not become 'gods' but actually, lost their place of dominion in exercising God's delegated authority and to share in His beautiful creation. God showed them who was really in charge by driving them out of the garden to till more difficult ground. In a sense, this was gracious on God's part because He made sure man had a chance of redemption, which could not happen if they had eaten the tree of life and lived forever in their sinful state.

Is it not ironic how low self-esteem has driven most people to only focus on the external and only what can be seen to boost self-confidence? However, this symptom of not focusing on inner beauty and reflecting God's glory, but wanting something else on the outside, has been with humanity ever since the fall of Adam.

3. **"You will not surely die"** – The devil managed to shift their attention from the immediate consequence which was spiritual death, that is, a separation and breaking of fellowship with God who is the source and breath of life.

4. **"Knowing good from evil"** – This was now direct assault on their selfish appetites. God had intended for man to be content in Him and live in the sufficiency of all the abundant provision at their disposal including the tree of life. The devil managed to tempt them on the one thing they were forbidden from eating, when they could live in the unlimited provision of what they were permitted to eat. In fact there is no record of God forbidding them from eating the tree of life as long as they obeyed God, and yet they allowed themselves to be blind-sided into eating the so called 'forbidden fruit' which was to protect them from themselves.

The result of befriending the enemy

Well we will have expected that the devil would deliver on his promises but instead, it was all disaster. This disaster is reproduced from Genesis 3 below:

"...So when the woman saw that the tree was good for food, and that it was a delight to the eyes, and that the tree was to be desired to make one wise, she took of its fruit and ate, and she also gave some to her husband who was with her, and he ate. Then the eyes of both were opened, and they knew that they were naked. And they sewed fig leaves together and made themselves loincloths. And they heard the sound of the LORD God walking in the garden in the cool of the day, and the man and his wife hid themselves from the presence of the LORD God"

This has been divided into three key parts and matched with a similar warning given by Apostle John in 1 John 2:15-16.

a. **John 2:16a; Lust of the flesh** – she perceived that the tree was good for food. Incidentally, God had given them many more trees for food but that was not enough for them.

b. **John 2:16b; Lust of the eyes** – she perceived that it was a delight to the eyes.

This was so false because God had already given them every tree that was a delight to the eyes, so there must have been even more beautiful trees for the purpose of delighting their eyes. Let me say this with all humility, bearing in mind that we should watch ourselves so we don't become tempted. I have always found it difficult to understand why a lot of people, especially the men will go behind their beautiful wives to commit adultery with 'less beautiful' women. Of course things are not as simple as that, because beauty can be subjective and as some will say, "it is in the eyes of the observer", whilst some spouses can be very difficult to live with. However, the lust of the eyes is real and we should remind ourselves daily not to live according to its desires.

c. **John 2:16c; Pride of life** – a tree to be desired to make one wise. The tree did not automatically make her wise. The devil managed to deceive her to desire it to make her wise, when in fact they had been endowed with so much wisdom from God. How could Adam have named all the animals with no prior knowledge (Genesis 2:18-19) if he did not already have wisdom from God? We must always beware of desires that are not of God but come out of selfish ambition, envy and jealousy, sheer competition and insecurity, because we might be dancing to the tune of the enemy, thinking he has your best interest at heart.

In summary, the devil tricked Adam and Eve to become **self-centred** instead of God centred; he tricked them into becoming **self-conscious** instead of God conscious and set them on a slippery slope of being **self-exalted** instead of submitting to the counsel of God. By that, he had managed to deceive them into committing the same sin he committed, by wanting to be God, for which he was cast out of heaven. As a result, they began to focus on their nakedness which they had always observed and began to hide from each other. They noticed their inadequacy and lost fellowship with God by hiding themselves from Him and seeking to salvage things themselves instead of seeking God's help.

Jesus' temptation (Matthew 4:3 – 10; Luke 4:1-13)

Before we discuss Jesus' temptation, let's note this important point: If you thought being a Christian was the end of your spiritual battles, think again. Jesus was actually sent into the midst of one of His most vicious direct spiritual conflicts by the Holy Spirit but He emerged victorious. Adam and Eve had failed miserably, by yielding to the three-fold temptation of the devil and thereby allowed sin and death to enter into the human race. Jesus, who was the second Adam, had to be made exactly like us so that in Him only can we have true freedom.

"Then Jesus was led by the Spirit into the wilderness to be tempted by the devil. After fasting forty days and forty nights, he was hungry. The tempter came to him and said, "If you are the Son of God, tell these stones to become bread." Jesus answered, "It is written: 'Man shall not live on bread alone, but on every word that comes from the mouth of God. Then the devil took him to the holy city and had him stand on the highest point of the temple. "If you are the Son of God," he said, "throw yourself down. For it is written: "He will command his angels concerning you, and they will lift you up in their hands, so that you will not strike your foot against a stone." Jesus answered him, "It is also written: 'Do not put the Lord your God to the test." Again, the devil took him to a very high mountain and showed him all the kingdoms of the world and their splendour. "All this I will give you," he said, "if you will bow down and worship me." Jesus said to him, "Away from me, Satan! For it is written: 'Worship the Lord your God, and serve him only."

Matthew 4:1-10

So the devil comes and says three things, all of which Jesus repels with the truth of scripture and by the help of the Holy Spirit:

    i. If you are the Son of God turn these stones into bread

ii.   If you are the Son of God throw yourself down
iii.   I will give you the kingdoms if you will bow down and
       worship me

A close examination of these statements from the devil, show a direct relationship to the temptation of Eve by the serpent in Genesis chapter 3. The devil challenged Eve's **identity** by saying you will become like God if you disobeyed. Here again, he challenges Christ on two occasions about His true identity of being the Son of God. The devil tried to shift His attention from being the Messiah who alone could save mankind but only through death on the cross, towards a material show down. Jesus Christ by the Spirit gained for us the victory which Adam and Eve failed to exercise over Satan in the garden. There are three categories of temptation Adam and Eve fell for. The world system, which is subject to the devil's devices, still uses these temptations against God's children today as outlined in 1 John 2:15-16, but which Jesus Christ overcame for us. The chart below summarises this nicely.

Genesis 3:1-13	Matthew 4: 1-10	1 John 2:15-16
The tree was good for food	Turn these stones to bread	The lust of the flesh
Pleasant to the eyes	The kingdoms and glory	The lust of the eyes
A tree to make one wise	Throw yourself down and show off	The pride of life

What was the devil's objective in all of these? You see, what Adam and Eve missed was the fact that the devil did not have their interest at heart but to be able to enthrone himself in the seat of their hearts and therefore their domain of jurisdiction which is the earth. When it comes to Jesus Christ, the devil goes for the jugular to reveal his true intentions by stating the conditions attached to everything we supposedly enjoy from him. "If you will bow down and worship me". This has always been his desire, the very reason for which he was cast out of heaven and this strong desire still remains. This is how he is described in the book of Isaiah.

"How you have fallen from heaven, morning star, son of the dawn! You have been cast down to the earth, you **who once laid low the**

nations! You said in your heart, "I will ascend to the heavens; I will raise my throne above the stars of God; I will sit enthroned on the mount of assembly, on the utmost heights of Mount Zaphon. I will ascend above the tops of the clouds; **I will make myself like the Most High.**" But you are brought down to the realm of the dead, to the depths of the pit. Those who see you stare at you, they ponder your fate: "Is this the **man who shook the earth and made kingdoms tremble, the man who made the world a wilderness, who overthrew its cities and would not let his captives go home?"**

Isaiah 14:12-17

The million dollar question is this; should the devil be our friend covertly or overtly? The answer is a resounding no. I have highlighted in bold the things he does for which he cannot be our friend. He lays low the nations, shakes the earth, makes kingdoms tremble, makes the world a wilderness and if you let him get you in his grip, he never lets go willingly. Our response should always be like that of Jesus, be gone, stay close to God and worship only Him because there is no middle ground.

With this background, we will use the rest of this book to explore the mission of Moses, God's servant, to free the children of Israel from bondage and Pharaoh's tricks at frustrating this divine mandate. I believe the devil still uses these same tricks or strategies today to make us live in defeat, guilt, regrets and depression and be unfulfilled in our walk with God and our worship of Him. As noted in the first chapter, "It was for freedom that Christ has set us free, no longer to be subject to a yoke of slavery". That is my ultimate aim for writing this book. It is not to glorify the devil, but to glorify God by exposing his deceptive schemes. We have been set free to worship, because God wants it that way and that is what this book intends to achieve.

I invite you to continue on this exciting journey to discover and appropriate the freedom, for which Christ died, was buried and on the third day resurrected into glory to prepare a place for us. God is seeking men and women who will worship Him in spirit and in truth, not half baked worship which only glorifies self and ultimately the devil. The devil desires it so badly, he dared to tempt Jesus to bow down and worship him for all the glories of this world. This is how critical the issues discussed in this book are, and I trust that by God, we will be victorious in our battle to overcome Satan's tricks and truly worship God in spirit and in truth because when we know and experience this truth, we will be free indeed. In the next chapter, we begin with the trick or trap of counterfeit offers, a form of carnal worship when we yield to them.

CHAPTER 3 COUNTERFEIT BARGAIN – CARNAL WORSHIP

"Pharaoh summoned Moses and Aaron and said, "Pray to the LORD to take the frogs away from me and my people, and **I will let your people go to offer sacrifices to the LORD**."

Exodus 8:8

"Then Pharaoh summoned Moses and Aaron. "This time I have sinned," he said to them. "The LORD is in the right, and I and my people are in the wrong. Pray to the LORD, for we have had enough thunder and hail. **I will let you go; you don't have to stay any longer**."

Exodus 9:27-28

"Freedom is never voluntarily given by the oppressor; it must be demanded by the oppressed"

Martin Luther King Jnr

If you have studied the history of oppressive systems and the liberation movements, you will note that it did not always come on a silver platter. The oppressor always holds on for as long as possible even when it is obvious the oppression needs to stop. These include the slave trade, colonisation, apartheid, occupations, inquisition, communism, religious oppression and racial discrimination. Before we go any further, it is important to look closely at God's detailed command to Moses which was the basis for his return to Egypt and which he repeated to Pharaoh.

"Afterward Moses and Aaron went to Pharaoh and said, "This is what the LORD, the God of Israel, says: '**Let my people go, so that they may hold a festival to me in the wilderness**." Pharaoh said, "Who is the LORD that I should obey him and let Israel go? I do not know the LORD and I will not let Israel go." Then they said, "The God of the Hebrews has met with us. Now let us take a three-day journey **into the wilderness to offer sacrifices to the LORD our God**".

These were Pharaoh's subsequent responses:
"Pharaoh summoned Moses and Aaron and said, "Pray to the LORD to take the frogs away from me and my people, and **I will let your people go to offer sacrifices to the LORD**."

Exodus 8:8

"Then Pharaoh summoned Moses and Aaron. "This time I have sinned," he said to them. "The LORD is in the right, and I and my people are in the wrong. Pray to the LORD, for we have had enough thunder and hail. **I will let you go; you don't have to stay any longer**."

Exodus 9:27-28

Pharaoh's counterfeit (half price) deals began here with these offers which were nothing but a vague expectation. He says I will let you go to offer sacrifices without saying where, the true intent of which becomes clearer in the ensuing chapters. On the second occasion, he vaguely said I will let you go, but without spelling out specifically, the purpose for letting them go. Though he mentions freedom and sacrifice, it was not the whole truth on both occasions. Prior to this, Pharaoh had tried to replicate God's miracles by the rod of Moses, through his magicians.

Now let us unpack this a bit more within the context of the Exodus narrative. It is important to remember that these were people who had been enslaved for over 400 years, had been trained, taught and conditioned all their lives to think, live and work as slaves. Therefore, any hint of freedom will be so welcome, they would have no time to evaluate critically and rationally, these half measures. When I was growing up, we used to sing this song, which I now believe to be unbiblical: "he that is down needs fear no fall". If you were thirsty or desperately hungry, even food from the rubbish bin, no matter how mouldy, will most likely to be appealing to you.

Perhaps a few examples will help us understand this concept. In the book of Genesis, (Genesis 25: 29 – 34) Esau was so hungry he despised his birth-right and sold it to Jacob for a bowl of lentil soup and used quite stark ignorant language, saying "I am at the point to die: and what profit shall this birth-right do to me? Unfortunately, however, the bible says he lost the blessing belonging to the Firstborn son as a result (Genesis chapter 27). In the story of Lazarus and the rich man (Luke 16: 19-31), we are told that the rich man who was "burning in hell" requested that Abraham asked Lazarus to give him a drop of water to quench his thirst. Of course the context was not about the drop of water, but in a literal sense, this was not possible. This is because a drop of water would be evaporated before it even reaches someone burning in fire. It just highlights his desperate need for help such that anything would do. The prodigal son, described in the gospels, was prepared to eat food left over by pigs, which for a Jew, is abominable, but he was desperate.

As a boy growing up, I saw people do things that look strange to me now based on where I live now. For example, used ('second hand') clothes such as braziers and underpants will never be passed on to charity shops in the UK or US to be sold or given away free of charge because we view them as unhygienic and not respecting human dignity. However, in the midst of poverty, especially in developing countries, I've seen people buy these things from second hand shops, which will never be the case if they could afford them. I have had debates with well-meaning Christians who live in the affluent culture of the West suggesting that it is ok for people in Africa to have low standards of living because they learn to cope and some actually use the bible to justify such abject poverty. The fact that we desire a better country provided by God in the life to come, is no excuse to let people wallow in such abject poverty and blatant indignity. It was such thinking that perpetuated evil schemes such as the slave trade for so long.

So here comes Moses, who rehearses God's instructions to Pharaoh and after the first few plagues, is promised by Pharaoh that they will be allowed to go to offer sacrifices in Exodus chapter 8. However, Pharaoh did not specifically say they could leave Egypt, the land of bondage. Then in chapter 9, he says you don't have to stay any longer without making reference to the sacrifice which is the worship of God for which God was instigating their freedom. In chapter 9, Pharaoh also leaves open, two options: 'leaving to make sacrifice' but more subtly, by saying 'you don't have to stay any longer'. This suggests, some or all of you have a choice to either leave or stay. Interestingly, future events in the wilderness journey will reveal how slavery had been ingrained into the mind-set of the Israelites, with devastating effects. Of course whilst slaves, they worked for the Pharaoh without receiving due wages and yet their food was guaranteed. The cucumbers and onions (which they later craved in the wilderness) of the nation's welfare pot was provided. As far as Pharaoh was concerned, they could still enjoy this 'comfort zone' within the borders of Egypt, which at best guaranteed their accommodation and food provisions, even if the Egyptians subjected them to hard labour. They needed a lot of faith to step out of this apparent security into the unknown and harsh realities of the desert and a place which God had said he was going to show to them.

Years before, God had thrown this same challenge to their forefather Abraham, by asking him to leave the security of his home, family and idolatry in Ur of the Chaldees into a land the Lord was going to show him (Genesis 12:1-3). This call represented a preaching of the gospel, which is the fact that in Jesus Christ, we all become the seed of Abraham, whether Jew or Gentile. Of course Abraham passed with distinction in spite of all his shortcomings, which included his tendency to tell lies and sometimes questioning God's faithfulness to carry him through. This promise to Abraham was not fulfilled in his lifetime even though Isaac, the promised heir arrived, and through whom the nation of Israel was eventually born. This promise of possessing the land of Canaan was about to be fulfilled in his offspring. However, they had to be willing to leave the slavery and certainty of Egypt which was bondage, into the uncertainty of being led by the pillar of cloud and fire through the desert into the promised land of Canaan, which required faith. That is why faith has sometimes been defined as risk, because it requires us to step out of the comfort and safety of our boat, if we want to walk on water.

What does it mean for you?
Before we answer this question, let us note this point, 'we should desire total, complete and absolute freedom as born again believers if we are to enjoy the benefits for which Christ died' even if other believers persecute you in the name of religion, dead tradition or false humility'. The reason is simple; "whom the Son (Jesus) shall set free,

is free indeed". If God says you can live holy and righteous, then let's believe we can and reckon ourselves dead to sin and alive to God in righteousness and not sugar coat it to justify our 'poverty' stricken Christianity. That is the doctrine of men which might not be evil or demonic but still falls far short of God's desire for our Christian walk of faith.

Therefore what this means for you is simply this; 'do not settle for counterfeit or half price measures, no matter how appealing, when there is a more glorious, complete, divine revelation and provision'. This counterfeit bargain or half price offer is what I've referred to in the chapter heading as carnal worship, because it promises much but delivers very little. Normal religion, including attending church meetings without living the life; replacing a genuine relationship with Jesus and the Holy Spirit with church activities and busyness are all dangerous half measures. We must be wary whatever we replace God with no matter how legitimate or religious it sounds. The Jews together with Aaron learnt a hard lesson later on by building the golden calf in Moses' absence.

Paul addressed the problem of carnal Christian worship when he chastised the church in Corinth, who allowed their perceived individual superstars to blur their vision of what their real calling was: They focused their attention so much on the messengers rather than the message of the cross.

"Brothers and sisters, I could not address you as people who live by the Spirit but as people who are still worldly—mere infants in Christ. I gave you milk, not solid food, for you were not yet ready for it. Indeed, you are still not ready. You are still worldly. For since there is jealousy and quarrelling among you, are you not worldly? Are you not acting like mere humans? For when one says, "I follow Paul," and another, "I follow Apollos," are you not mere human beings? What, after all, is Apollos? And what is Paul? Only servants, through whom you came to believe - as the Lord has assigned to each his task. I planted the seed, Apollos watered it, but God has been making it grow. So neither the one who plants nor the one who waters is anything, but only God, who makes things grow. The one who plants and the one who waters have one purpose, and they will each be rewarded according to their own labour. For we are co-workers in God's service; you are God's field, God's building. By the grace God has given me, I laid a foundation as a wise builder, and someone else is building on it. But each one should build with care. For no one can lay any foundation other than the one already laid, which is Jesus Christ".

1 Corinthians 3: 1-10

Carnal worship has five basic characteristics according to Paul:

i. Worldly tendencies, i.e. leaving the world system physically and in word but not renewed in our minds and our thinking.

ii. Immaturity: not growing and developing because of slave mentality and feeding on milk which only belongs to babies,

iii. Church cliques and disunity: forgetting that there are many parts of the body with different gifts and functions but the same faith, same Spirit, same Lord and same hope,

iv. Walks in the flesh – jealousy and quarrelling,

v. Does not have Christ as its foundation but traditions, personality cults, denominationalism, elitism and competition for recognition.

In chapter 2 of first Corinthians, Paul spells out the characteristics of the true spiritual man. He reveals the things God has prepared for those who love Him, which He wanted them to enjoy, but which they had missed and instead focused on lighter matters that were of no consequence to their relationship with God. They had fallen for the trap of counterfeit, carnal spirituality built around outward appearance rather than inward transformation. We need to overcome this barrier and when you have overcome it, do not rest, because the bargain gets tougher and more subtle as Pharaoh throws another spanner into the mix by tempting Moses to compromise which we want to explore in the next chapter.

CHAPTER 4 COMPROMISE BARGAIN – DILUTE WORSHIP

"And the LORD said to Moses, "Rise early in the morning and stand before Pharaoh as he comes out to the water. Then say to him, thus says the LORD: Let My people go, that they may serve Me. Or else, if you will not let my people go, behold, I will send swarms of flies on you and your servants, on your people and into your houses. The houses of the Egyptians shall be full of swarms of flies, and also the ground on which they stand. And in that day I will set apart the land of Goshen, in which my people dwell, that no swarms of flies shall be there, in order that you may know that I am the LORD in the midst of the land. I will make a difference between my people and your people. Tomorrow this sign shall be. And the LORD did so. Thick swarms of flies came into the house of Pharaoh, into his servants' houses, and into all the land of Egypt. The land was corrupted because of the swarms of flies. **Then Pharaoh called for Moses and Aaron, and said**, "**Go, sacrifice to your God in the land**." And Moses said, **it is not right to do so**, for we would be sacrificing the abomination of the Egyptians to the LORD our God. If we sacrifice the abomination of the Egyptians before their eyes, then will they not stone us? **We will go three days' journey into the wilderness and sacrifice to the LORD our God as He will command us**."

Exodus 8: 20-27

In normal diplomatic negotiations, both sides begin with a standard set of demands and negotiate towards an outcome that is acceptable to both parties and which they could reasonably live with. It normally represents the minimum any party is willing to accept without jeopardising their key interests. This requires either side(s) to compromise, and follows the principle of win-win and in most cases, either side has so called red lines which they usually are unwilling to cross. There are two things to mention quickly from this approach before we get deeper into the subject of this chapter:

    a.   Firstly, the devil does not believe in a win-win. He only desires the whole thing and only gives bait that will eventually damage our interests. Pharaoh's backing out of most of the agreements is enough evidence he had no interest in negotiating a settlement. Therefore never enter into any diplomacy with the devil. Jesus never did, his final words after being tempted was "be gone from me devil".

b. The best deal from the devil is far worse than God's minimum. We need not give any ground because there is no minimum we can live with. Jesus Christ has already defeated him and paid the price for this outcome so he has no bargaining rights.

Now back to the main story. Pharaoh calls Moses and as noted in the verses above, offers him only half of the demands. These were not Moses' terms of negotiation but God's absolute instructions and commandments for their total freedom. Pharaoh agreed to allow them to go sacrifice but guess where he wanted them to sacrifice. He offered the land of Egypt, the very place of their slavery, bondage and oppression. Instead of 100% he gives 50% which is after all better than the 0% he offered at the beginning. This was dilute worship. Note that in those days, worship involved both the act (sacrifice) as well as the place of worship. Both were non-negotiable and Pharaoh wanted them to compromise on this instruction from God. This was so important that later on, God will instruct Moses to build a tabernacle where his presence, represented by the Ark of the Covenant will dwell and where the priests will come to offer sacrifices on behalf of the people. Furthermore, God subsequently instructed them to build the temple through Solomon (1 Kings 5: 1 – 6) and after it had been destroyed, commanded it's rebuilding through Ezra and Zerubbabel (Ezra 1: 1 - 2; Zechariah 4: 1 – 14) and chastised them through the prophet Haggai for building their own homes whilst God's temple laid in ruins (Haggai 1: 1 - 8).

The woman of Samaria told Jesus in John chapter 4 that "our fathers worshipped on this mountain". She was obviously referring to the Samaritans' place of worship in contrast to the Jewish place of worship at Jerusalem. Even today, in Israel, the Wailing Wall is held as one of their most holy sites. In fact many religions still hold on dearly to this principle of holy sites where people go to worship their form of deity and any desecration of such places is regarded tantamount to sacrilege. Pharaoh wanted them to sing the Lord's song in a strange land.

However, in New Testament terms we are to worship in spirit and in truth without any imbalance like Pharaoh wanted them to do. It involved both substance and essence. We cannot be equally yoked with the world and think we can make an effective impact. Whilst we must seek to engage unbelievers with the gospel, there can be no fellowship between light and darkness, believer and unbeliever or between Christ and Belial. Now, it needs to be made clear that this does not in any way imply we have no interaction, because I've seen some Christians take this message to undesirable extremes. All it means is that we need to make contact without contamination. The devil will allow you to perform religious rituals as long as you remain in his camp. Jesus saved us all the way and we are to worship as the Lord commands.

Is less better?

Architect Ludwig Mies van der Rohe used the phrase "Less is more" to describe the aesthetic strategy of arranging the various components of a building to create an impression of extreme simplicity, by enlisting every element and detail to serve multiple visual and functional purposes. A typical example is the use of waste hot water to generate heating for rooms and buildings. In "less is more" situations, the idea is that you will have a greater impact on whatever the expected outcome is, by limiting the presentation to just the bare essentials needed to convey the message or idea. In certain scientific analytical techniques, very high concentrations of a given compound of interest can cause saturation of the instrument's detector which results in recording of false values.

The basic principle of the phrase is that simplicity and clarity lead to good design which appears somewhat laudable and even biblical in terms of modesty, as Paul clearly outlined in Philippians. However, taken too far, the 'less is more' or rather 'less is better' philosophy can become a trap for falling into all kinds of behaviour which we try to justify even when it goes against the truth of scripture. For example, we may allege that no one is an angel and therefore should be left to compromise on integrity. We can easily say, after all no man is perfect so it's ok to continue in my sin without seeking to be transformed on the inside. How many of us (emphasis 'us') have rationalized certain wrong habits we picked up whilst growing up using statements such as "this is just who I am and you take it or leave it"? Of course we are to love people unconditionally, but none of us will encourage or allow our children to play with naked fire under the guise of unconditional love. When and if they do get burnt, we comfort and dress their burns but never send them straight back to the fire again. It's so easy to accept the so called 'soft sins' such as insecurity, jealousy, envy, gossip, materialism and gluttony whilst condemning fornication, abortion, homosexuality and adultery. However, the blunt truth is that all of these are listed as works of the flesh in Galatians 5. The challenging question we must all confront is this; "will you be able to argue your case and justify gossip or so called soft sin, if God were standing right in front of you? Put another way, will we accept anger, verbal abuse and violence from someone because they justify it on the basis of just who they were?

Whilst, we should be for simplicity, it should never be at the expense of compromising on God's truth and his promises. In the discovery and development of new drugs and therapies, patient safety is almost always non-negotiable and the pharmaceutical industry and regulators go to great lengths to ensure and prove the safety of every medicine as part of regulatory approval processes. This is necessary to reduce the chances of drug toxicity in patients which causes serious side effects and sometimes death. Medicines and even food that do not meet prescribed standards including wrong packaging, get removed from circulation. In recent years, there has been the reported scandal across Europe and the UK where horse DNA has been detected in food products labelled as beef. The experts and politicians all agree there was no direct or immediate risk to human health but was an issue of deception in packaging and labelling. However, that was still enough to cause all affected products to be withdrawn from several supermarket shelves. If human beings expect and demand such high standards of safety and quality, why should we expect God to require less?

Our response
We began this chapter using the common diplomatic objective of

'win-win' which is of course useful. However, Pharaoh's intention was: 'I give one and take one, which amounts to nothing. The issue is not whether it is 'win-win' but rather whether we will live in absolute or partial obedience, which should be our measuring stick. Moses' response to Pharaohs proposal is therefore very revealing and should inform how we respond to such temptation.

And Moses said, "It is not right to do so ... We will go three days' journey into the wilderness and sacrifice to the LORD our God as He will command us."

Exodus 8:26-27

Though the debate between Moses and Pharaoh was about where to sacrifice to the Lord, the issue at stake was more than geography. The reason is found right at the very end of verse 27 where Moses states "as He will command us". It's about obedience and trust in God's instructions. Their future and continuous worship and relationship with God was dependent upon and guaranteed by taking the first step out of Egypt. Could our inability to hear and discern God's voice and direction for our lives be linked to the fact that we have not obeyed the original prompting by the Holy Spirit in the first place? Are we looking for great things when we have not been faithful in the little things? God has a plan and bright future for us but requires us to go on a journey of faith and trust. You may not have a Pharaoh refusing to let you go on this journey. It could well be your friends and family, employer or even pastor, who keeps you stagnant and stuck in one place and prevent you from advancing in God's plan for your life. It might well be your own fears, insecurities, comparison with others and desire to be in absolute control, that make you settle for what is less than God's vision for your life. Do not compromise by disobeying, but be like Moses and be prepared to step out in faith, trusting that God will say to you
"... This is the way, walk ye in it".

CHAPTER 5 COMMITMENT BARGAIN – MIXED WORSHIP
(Exodus 8:28)

"There's a difference between interest and commitment. When you're interested in doing something, you do it only when it's convenient. When you're committed to something, you accept no excuses - only results."

Kenneth Blanchard

Pharaoh said, "I will let you go to offer sacrifices to the LORD your God in the wilderness, **but you must not go very far**. Now pray for me."

Exodus 8:28

"Sin is not your friend, it has never been and never will".

Joshua Boateng (author)

As the discussions continued, Pharaoh intensifies his tricks and gets really subtle as God intensified the plagues. In seeking to prevent the Israelites from obtaining absolute freedom, Pharaoh now attacks their commitment, which many great heroes have fallen victim to. He addresses Moses' objections from the previous chapter by offering them the two key demands i.e. freedom to go sacrifice and to do so outside of Egypt in the wilderness. However, he attempts to insert a 'hook' that can be easily missed if we read too quickly. He says to Moses, have all you want, but **do not go very far**. What did he mean by that? Well his motives could be several things. The primary one was encouraging the children of Israel to serve and follow God from a distance, not going all the way, leaving room for possible backsliding into Egypt. He could also have meant, you can get into the motions of religious activity in the best cathedrals, wear the best clothes, enjoy the most organised worship services, indulge in the best theological arguments and still not go far in God because they did not press into God by hungering and thirsting for more of Him and for God to have all of them. I remember a song we sang in Sunday school as a kid, "I have decided to follow Jesus, no turning back". Like Peter, Pharaoh tried to make them follow God at a distance and is recorded in the first three gospels and proves its significance.

"But **Peter followed him (i.e. Jesus) at a distance**, right up to the courtyard of the high priest. He entered and sat down with the guards to see the outcome"

Matthew 26:58

"**Peter followed him (i.e. Jesus) at a distance**, right into the courtyard of the high priest. There he sat with the guards and warmed himself at the fire"

Mark 14:54

"Then seizing him, they led him away and took him (i.e. Jesus) into the house of the high priest. **Peter followed at a distance**"

Luke 22:54

If we yield to Pharaoh's suggestion of not going too far, we will follow Jesus from a distance, and by a slow process, could end up denying the Saviour like Peter did. Pastor Joel DeSelm[1] of Woodburn Missionary Church, in his blog on the theme of 'Peter following from a distance', notes the following:

"...Now the case can be made that Peter was showing great loyalty. That his stealth and careful plotting allowed him to infiltrate the "enemy's camp" in order to keep an eye on Jesus. To be sure he seemed to be doing more and showing greater concern for Jesus' well-being than the rest of the disciples! On the other hand, Peter did deny the Lord not once but three times. As I pondered the gospel narratives I kept coming back to this idea of "following from a distance." How easy it is to get caught into that trap. Of course I can justify "why" I sometimes follow Jesus from a distance just like Peter could have justified his actions that night as well. I have all kinds of reasons, explanations, and rationalizations why "following at a distance" is sometimes a good thing to do. The reality? It's not. It's never good to follow Jesus "from a distance. When I follow at a distance I lose contact with Jesus. I'm not able to talk with Him nor listen to Him as well. Following at a distance tends to cause me to rely upon my own wisdom, "hunches," and ideas. And often they aren't the best. But the biggest downside to following at a distance is this: it can quickly lead to denying the Lord. Don't believe me? Ask Peter."[1]

Here was Peter, who had vowed previously to never let Jesus go to the cross and was prepared to die for him. Of course, we must put this in perspective, because Peter, left all to follow Jesus. As a Jew, he will most likely have entertained thoughts of Jesus being the Messiah who will deliver Israel from the oppression of Rome and here he was, all his dreams had come crashing down. What will he and his friends go to tell their wives and families? Were those three years spent in vain? What about the miracles, the signs and wonders, all the lovely parables and teachings? Despite this rich heritage and experience of walking with Jesus side by side, Peter at the last minute had his hopes dashed and therefore followed Jesus Christ from a distance. These are all strong possibilities but quite speculative as the bible does not definitively say so. However, the true answer can be found in Luke's gospel:

"Simon, Simon, Satan has asked to sift all of you as wheat. But I have prayed for you, Simon that your faith may not fail. And when you have turned back, strengthen your brothers. But he replied, Lord, I am ready to go with you to prison and to death. Jesus answered, I tell you, Peter, before the rooster crows today, you will deny three times that you know me."

Luke 22:31-34

Jesus had already foreseen the level of satanic attack that His followers will come under, but particularly against Peter, who will be given the responsibility of leading the early New Testament church. He came in for the most vicious of these attacks, being tempted to deny Jesus Christ three times. How will Satan achieve this, except by the slow process of following from a distance? He could have stayed away like the other disciples who were all scattered for fear of the mob. However, we can be rest assured, Jesus had prayed for them all. Again this prayer can be found in John 17 where the real "Lord's Prayer" is found. Here Jesus prayed for them and all believers, that none will be lost by remaining in him and him in us just as He was one with the Father.

"I pray for them. I am not praying for the world, but for those you have given me, for they are yours. All I have is yours, and all you have is mine. And glory has come to me through them. I will remain in the world no longer, but they are still in the world, and I am coming to you. Holy Father, protect them by the power of your name, the name you gave me, so that they may be one as we are one. While I was with them, I protected them and kept them safe by that name you gave me. None has been lost except the one doomed to destruction so that Scripture would be fulfilled. I am coming to you now, but I say these things while I am still in the world, so that they may have the full measure of my joy within them. I have given them your word and the world has hated them, for they are not of the world any more than I am of the world. My prayer is not that you take them out of the world but that you protect them from the evil one. They are not of the world, even as I am not of it. Sanctify them by the truth; your word is truth. As you sent me into the world, I have sent them into the world. For them I sanctify myself, that they too may be truly sanctified. My prayer is not for them alone. I pray also for those who will believe in me through their message, that all of them may be one, Father, just as you are in me and I am in you. May they also be in us so that the world may believe that you have sent me. I have given them the glory that you gave me, that they may be one as we are one. I in them and you in me - so that they may be brought to complete unity. Then the world will know that you sent me and have loved them even as you have loved me. Father, I want those you have given me to be with me where I am, and to see my glory, the glory you have given me because you loved me before the creation of the world. Righteous Father, though the world does not know you, I know you, and they know that you have sent me. [26] I have made you known to them, and will continue to make you known in order that the love you have for me may be in them and that I myself may be in them."

The second typical example of someone who fell victim to this dangerous bargain in the bible was Lot. The background to his story is that after prospering and increasing in wealth through his association with Abraham, conflict breaks out between their servants. Abraham in his maturity, allows Lot to choose the best land so they could separate and not be in conflict any more, given that they were family. Lot pitched his tent near Sodom after separating from Abraham. Now if you read it too quickly, it sounds very innocuous but the significant words here are "**near**" and "**Sodom**". Sodom was full of evil and wickedness and Lot had no business pitching his tent near Sodom. This was very similar to Pharaoh's suggestion that Moses and his people should not go too far away into the wilderness. However, the next time we hear of Lot, he was **not near** Sodom but actually **within** Sodom and eventually captured by invading armies and had to be rescued by Abraham. However, he paid a heavy price for going near Sodom and ending up inside, because it cost him his wife in the process (Genesis 13:12, 14:11-12). Matters got worse for him because afterwards, he unknowingly committed incest twice. Lot was made drunk by his own daughters and then both went ahead to sleep with him. I imagine the daughters will have learnt these evil ways from living inside of Sodom. The result of these two acts of abomination was Ammon (Ammonites) and Moab (Moabites), two nations who constantly tormented the Jews throughout the time of Moses and the kings of Israel. This is how serious the issue of following God and Jesus Christ from a distance can be.

Cain's warning

This bargain is so important, because it is probably the one that seems least harmful and yet very deadly. Before we wrap it up, let's have a brief look at Cain and how he came to kill his brother because it is set around worship and sacrifice, the main reason why God wanted to set the children of Israel free. Damage to the relationship between Cain and God ultimately led him to kill his brother. Before you jump with religious hypocrisy to judge Cain as a murderer, think again because, unfortunately we have all murdered at one point or the other, at least with our tongues. Let's read Genesis again from the Living Bible translation.

"Abel became a shepherd, while Cain was a farmer. At harvest time Cain brought the Lord a gift of his farm produce, and Abel brought the fatty cuts of meat from his best lambs, and presented them to the Lord. And the Lord accepted Abel's offering, but not Cain's. This made Cain both dejected and very angry, and his face grew dark with fury. "Why are you angry?" the Lord asked him. Why is your face so dark with rage? It can be bright with joy if you will do what you should! But if you refuse to obey, watch out. **Sin is waiting to attack you, longing to destroy you**. But you can conquer it! One day Cain suggested to his brother, let's go out into the fields. And while they were together there, Cain attacked and killed his brother. But afterwards the Lord asked Cain, Where is your brother? Where is Abel? How should I know? Cain retorted. Am I supposed to keep track of him wherever he goes? But the Lord said, your brother's blood calls to me from the ground. What have you done?"

Genesis 4: 2-10

We need to challenge ourselves about the hidden conflicts in our hearts (some from childhood) which eat at us, saps our spiritual energy and destroy our relationships with God and subsequently with others. These include anger, offense, bitterness, jealousy, envy and unforgiveness. These are little foxes that destroy the vine of fellowship with God and with others. They are mainly heart sins, which singing, taking communion, speaking in tongues and engaging in church activity are not enough to deal with. Only brute acknowledgment before God and repentance will do. If we don't, we will most likely follow Christ at a distance, become isolated and make ourselves easy prey for the enemy to attack us. Before we go on, let us remind ourselves of the following defining statement:

"Sin is not your friend, has never been and never will".

The key consequence of Cain not bringing the right sacrifice was his anger, jealousy, hatred of his brother, unrepentance and finally murder. Cain's offering was rejected; he got angry, was given a second chance and yet did nothing about it. God said; "Sin lies at the door of your heart, its desire is to have you". What sin? The same sin committed by his parents i.e. disobeying God's commands. It is quite clear from verse 7 of Genesis chapter4, that Cain knew what offering God expected him to bring to make him and his sacrifice acceptable so he could have joy. Why did Cain murder his brother? The same spirit of evil and the deception of Satan were at work against Cain. How do we know? Let's read 1 John 3 vs 11-16 and Jude 1 vs 11, 16. The answer is because he sided with the devil and did not choose God's way by his actions. Even after killing Abel, Cain could not care an inch about his brother's welfare when God asked him.

"For this is the message you heard from the beginning: We should love one another. Do not be like Cain, who belonged to the evil one and murdered his brother. And why did he murder him? Because his own actions were evil and his Abel's were righteous. Do not be surprised, my brothers and sisters, if the world hates you. We know that we have passed from death to life, because we love each other. Anyone who does not love remains in death. Anyone who hates a brother or sister is a murderer, and you know that no murderer has eternal life residing in him. This is how we know what love is: Jesus Christ laid down his life for us. And we ought to lay down our lives for our brothers and sisters."

1 John 3: 11 - 16

"Woe to them! They have taken the way of Cain; these people are grumblers and faultfinders; they follow their own evil desires; they boast about themselves and flatter others for their own advantage."

Jude 1: 11a, 16

Therefore, sin is not our friend, we only need to flee and not play around it, because like fire, it is bound to burn us, no matter how long it might take. We need to be fully cut off from every cord of evil within the worldly system. God has provided a full salvation, let's dip fully into it and live the abundant life for which Christ saved us. If we are to survive, and to please the Lord, let us serve Him wholeheartedly, spirit, soul and body, not haphazardly and with excuses all the time.

One of the strongest statements ever made in the bible can be found in the message of Jesus Christ through John, the beloved apostle, to the church in Laodicea.

"To the angel of the church in Laodicea write: These are the words of the Amen, the faithful and true witness, the ruler of God's creation. **I know your deeds, that you are neither cold nor hot. I wish you were either one or the other! So, because you are lukewarm - neither hot nor cold - I am about to spit you out of my mouth.** You say, I am rich; I have acquired wealth and do not need a thing. But you do not realize that you are wretched, pitiful, poor, blind and naked. I counsel you to buy from me gold refined in the fire, so you can become rich; and white clothes to wear, so you can cover your shameful nakedness; and salve to put on your eyes, so you can see. Those whom I love I rebuke and discipline. So be earnest and repent. Here I am! I stand at the door and knock. If anyone hears my voice and opens the door, I will come in and eat with that person, and they with me. To the one who is victorious, I will give the right to sit with me on my throne, just as I was victorious and sat down with my Father on his throne. Whoever has ears, let them hear what the Spirit says to the churches."

Revelation 3:14 - 22

These are very strong words from the glorified Saviour of the world and the key complaint was being lukewarm, which is a subtle form of non-commitment. Solomon said in one of his books, the Songs of Solomon, "catch the little foxes that destroy the vine". The enemy does not always attack in an obvious and expected fashion. As long as he can sow a negative seed, it is so difficult to detect and he does not care how much religious activity we engage in, he will have planted a dangerous bargain without us even knowing. We therefore need to be very discerning and vigilant.

CHAPTER 6 commUnity BARGAIN – DIVIDED WORSHIP
(Exodus 10: 7-12)

"Behold how good and lovely it is when brethren dwell in unity. For there the Lord commands His blessing."

Psalm 133

Up to this point Pharaoh has failed to side track Moses and Aaron from their mission and vision to free the Israelites from bondage. But now, he throws in another poison which has killed many a strong family, marriage, organisation or church by going after their unity of purpose. He says enjoy worship as God wants, not from a distance, not diluted, nor counterfeit. Actually he's happy if you get so insular you start to think you're the only local church in the community and the only church or denomination able to save mankind. I could imagine him saying, bask in Pentecostal charismatic power; put lots of effort into spreading evangelical orthodoxy, exercise your minds in apologetic reasoning to defend the faith, engage in theological scholarship to understand and explain God in more complicated ways and only find fault with other people's theology; study to show yourself approved unto God, but do all these important aspects of the church in discord and disunity. Pharaoh somehow implies all these with the statement "... **only the men should go without the women and children**". Before we move on, let me make this statement which I picked up from a leadership / team building website.

"Teamwork is intentional not accidental".

In the same way, unity is deliberate and intentional, not by accident because it is a difficult enterprise, but also a rewarding one if we are prepared to pay the price. Of course, I'm not speaking of unity at any price. Recent happenings including child abuse cases in certain church quarters have been overlooked instead of being addressed which has been a source of great shame to the body of Christ. Pharaoh is very cunning because the question must be asked; why was he pulling all these strings, given the fact that the men will have been the major source of his slave labour? It is quite obvious if you scratch the surface, because in the Middle Eastern culture of the day, the men were the bread winners and as heads of the families, were responsible for the well-being of their wives, children and unmarried sisters. Therefore, it is clear that they were bound to come back to Egypt which will have made their freedom of no consequence. In fact, it will have been no different to worshipping God from a distance. Those of us who hail from countries with former colonial masters, know how dependent most of those countries are on their former colonisers. In fact a lot of them are easily blackmailed and threatened with cutting of aid and economic sanctions if certain of their demands are not met. That is not real independence and it must be challenged. For example, the policy of using foreign aid as a pretext to allow cheap foreign goods into developing countries which prevents them from competing effectively is unfair in my opinion. It is always laudable to help to the poor by providing fish, but it is even better to teach them to fish for themselves as that is more sustainable. For more on the social implications of aid dependency and the need for responsibility to secure true freedom, please refer to the excellent book by the late Dr Myles Munroe of blessed memory, entitled "The Burden of Freedom"[2].

Now let's examine a few manifestations of disunity and divided worship.

1. Denominationalism

This can manifest itself in several ways including sectarianism and elitism. For example, it's common to hear many groups and preachers, so puffed up with knowledge make statements such as "we are solid on the word and doctrine" compared to others who only engage in emotionalism. Whilst I believe, correct interpretation and handling of doctrine should form the foundation of any church movement, this should primarily be about the essentials, in particular, centred on the person and work of Christ. We must be very careful not to hold others in contempt out of denominational elitism. I lived in Glasgow for six years and was always sad at seeing the level of animosity between Celtic and Rangers fans which did not just remain football rivalry but spilled over into perceived Catholic and

Protestant conflict. It is interesting but also very sad that a political struggle has been extended in the Northern Ireland conflict to be about Catholic IRA and the Protestant Unionists. There is no biblical justification for this and probably why countries such as the United States and France are aggressive in their secular policy of separation between church and state. It is quite interesting to find people who will choose to stay home and in some cases backslide, when they move abroad or to another town if they cannot find a church belonging to their 'denomination'.

2. Racism

Related to denominationalism is the issue of racism which is obviously a very sensitive subject, and therefore needs to be addressed sensitively. Some Christians will only attend a church of their colour or race, which are dangerous attitudes to have in my opinion. Of course we need to balance this by appreciating that sometimes, this might be necessary for purposes of language convenience and effective communication, but the objective is always towards a unity of purpose and focus on Christ. Here I will like to reproduce an interview given by Pastor Rodriguez[3], a well-known Hispanic preacher and pastor of a large church in the United States of America.

"My mission in life is to reconcile the vertical and the horizontal. I believe the cross is both righteousness and justice, sanctification and service, covenant and community, orthodoxy and orthopraxy. It is both John 3:16 and Matthew 25, conviction and compassion, truth and love. It is Billy Graham's message and Dr King's march. My mission in life is to speak to a church, speak to a generation. To try to frame the optics of a movement that stands centred not in the extremes but in the centre of the cross, where righteousness meets justice, where we reconcile the optics of redemption with the metrics of reconciliation. That, I believe, is the strongest part of the cross, the nexus, and the point of convergence. And that's my mission. I call that the Lamb's agenda". In response to the following question, he gave this prophetic answer, provided in italics

Question: "As the Hispanic church continues to grow, it will naturally exert increasing influence over the American church. How would a surging Hispanic church reshape the American religious landscape"?

Answer: "Number one, the American church will be more holistic. It will reconcile the vertical and the horizontal. It will reconcile the Way with the Dream. As a result of the Hispanic church, this generation of American Christians and the next generation will sing "There Is Room at the Cross" and "We Shall Overcome."

The second way the Hispanic church will impact the American church is multi-ethnicity. Little by little over the next 20 years, Sunday morning's segregation will become something more of an anomaly. Latinos are not a race. We are an ethnicity, a conglomeration. We are the convergence of the African experience, if you're a Latino from the Caribbean. Or the Spaniard/European experience, the white. Or the Asian Indian—the native from the Incas, the Aztecs, the Mayans. Hispanics are the walking United Nations. And because of that, we want our churches to look like us. We want our churches to be black, brown, white and yellow. Which means we're going to see an explosion of multi-ethnic churches in America pastored by English speaking Latinos. We repudiate the idea of cultural or ethnic myopia. We're pushing back on that. So the church will become more diverse in its expression. We will look like the kingdom of God, his mosaic, God's tapestry.

3. Old versus young

In the interview above, Pastor Rodriguez continued with this quote which addresses effectively, the next fault line of division within the body of Christ and even in society, i.e. the generational gap.

"Number three, Latinos are known for la familia. If you look at our families, you will see Grandma and Grandpa living with Mom and Dad. You will see two or three generations living in a house. We're known for that. La familia. It's the ethos of the community. We transfer that to the church. So the churches are not just Abraham churches; you're going to see Abraham, Isaac, Jacob and Joseph attending our churches, three or four generations in one church worshipping Christ together[3]".

"There has been an explosion of Hispanic mega churches over the past 10 years alone. In 2000 you could count the number of Hispanic mega churches maybe on two hands. One decade later, you will now find a Hispanic mega church in every major Hispanic population area. And these are not just Hispanic mega churches; these are Hispanic mega churches that get the vertical and horizontal. These are holistic churches, and they integrate first, second, third generations. Some of them have Spanish services, some of them English services, and some also offer bilingual services, so Mom and Dad and the children can worship together. They're going beyond Latino and they're reaching everyone in their community, lending to the rise in Hispanic-led multi-ethnic churches."

This generational divide exists either by way of age and experiencing different moves of God. It can manifest itself as a preference for hymns by older people as against love for modern choruses by younger people. Some prefer slow and so called worship songs against fast praise songs both of which are not biblical because slow does not mean worship neither does fast mean praise. We must not forget that the devil also seeks worship because he requested that of Jesus and the more time we spend debating methods and styles of worship, rather than worshipping in Spirit, the more Satan enjoys our worship which belongs only to God. Even the King James and NIV versions of the bible can be a source of division which makes the devil really happy.

I have heard very spiritual and experienced Christian leaders condemn songs that were composed out of the writer's personal encounter and relationship with God because it did not contain enough theology and doctrine. Such a line of reasoning, though borne out of noble intent, is quite flawed because the biggest song book in the bible, the Psalms has a lot of highly charged emotions put to song, especially by David. Of course, David also penned some of the best known messianic Psalms which spoke of the coming, suffering, burial and resurrection of Jesus Christ, as found in Psalms 22 to 24. Furthermore, the teaching in scripture is that doctrine is taught and therefore must be learnt and studied. If we want to know more doctrine, then we've got to study by reading the bible, books and commentaries. If songs help us remember doctrine, that is brilliant, but please let's not destroy community by imposing our expectations on others when there is little or no support from scripture. Of course the opposite is also true; just because you had an experience with God in a particular area or season does not make it a general dogma which everybody must follow and when they do not, they get labelled unspiritual and old fashioned. Both these extremes can be found in the church and are not edifying in the sight of God. It is a Pharaoh bargain, designed to cause disunity and restrict our freedoms in Christ which should not be restricted to mechanics of religion and traditional rites.

4. Competition and critical spirit

It is so easy to critique other people's methods and ministry emphasis. Some people never win souls and yet have enough audacity to spend all their time analysing how another groups evangelistic activities do not match their standards. How can we talk about standards when we sit there doing nothing? Such an attitude tends to result in intolerance which Jesus always discouraged. We stand the risk of appearing before God crownless because we spent all our time finding out and dissecting other people's faults. The clearest example of this can be found in the gospels of Mark and Luke which are quoted below.

"They came to Capernaum. When he was in the house, he asked them, what were you arguing about on the road? But they kept quiet because on the way they had argued about who was the greatest. Sitting down, Jesus called the Twelve and said, anyone who wants to be first must be the very last, and the servant of all. He took a little child whom he placed among them. Taking the child in his arms, he said to them, whoever welcomes one of these little children in my name welcomes me; and whoever welcomes me does not welcome me but the one who sent me. Whoever Is Not Against Us Is for Us. Teacher, said John, **we saw someone driving out demons in your name and we told him to stop, because he was not one of us. Do not stop him, Jesus said. For no one who does a miracle in my name can in the next moment say anything bad about me, for whoever is not against us is for us**. Truly I tell you, anyone who gives you a cup of water in my name because you belong to the Messiah will certainly not lose their reward".   Mark 9: 33 - 41

"An argument started among the disciples as to which of them would be the greatest. Jesus, knowing their thoughts, took a little child and made him stand beside him. Then he said to them, whoever welcomes this little child in my name welcomes me; and whoever welcomes me welcomes the one who sent me. For it is the one who is least among you all who is the greatest. Master, said John, **we saw someone driving out demons in your name and we tried to stop him, because he is not one of us. Do not stop him, Jesus said, for whoever is not against you is for you**".

Luke 9: 46 - 50

It is interesting that this story about John competing with others was told within the context of humility, where Jesus taught that the least is actually the greatest. The more we gloat about our way of doing things, compared to others, the smaller and proud we appear in the sight of God. More interestingly, the account of the incident described by Mark happened soon after Peter, James and John had witnessed the amazing sight of Jesus being transfigured into His heavenly glory. Of course, it is not surprising that they were so set in their ways because when God wanted them to listen to Jesus' words, they were so mesmerised by the sight, that in Matthew's account, it is recorded that these three disciples wanted to build a monument and remain on the mountain instead of getting on with the task of spreading the gospel message.

What about the Old Testament? You will have thought that men such as Joshua who had witnessed some of the events in Egypt will have learnt this lesson, but when it came to scratch, he was found wanting. This is how Moses records a typical example of this kind of disunity in the book of Numbers:

"The LORD answered Moses, Is the LORD's arm too short? Now you will see whether or not what I say will come true for you. So Moses went out and told the people what the LORD had said. He brought together seventy of their elders and made them stand round the tent. Then the LORD came down in the cloud and spoke with him, and he took some of the power of the Spirit that was on him and put it on the seventy elders. When the Spirit rested on them, they prophesied – but did not do so again. **However, two men, whose names were**

Eldad and Medad, had remained in the camp. They were listed among the elders, but did not go out to the tent. Yet the Spirit also rested on them, and they prophesied in the camp. A young man ran and told Moses, Eldad and Medad are prophesying in the camp. Joshua son of Nun, who had been Moses' assistant since youth, spoke up and said, Moses, my lord, stop them! But Moses replied, are you jealous for my sake? I wish that all the LORD's people were prophets and that the LORD would put his Spirit on them! Then Moses and the elders of Israel returned to the camp".

Numbers 11: 23 - 30

The punchline is that we should not criticise when we do not understand what is going on beyond our natural experience and not get into a battle on behalf of God, which He never asked us to fight in the first place.

5. Clergy versus laity

This is a particularly huge problem in the church historically and one that is dear to my heart. I have covered the dangers of such attitude in chapter two of my previous book, "The Apprentice: Empowered to Impact Your World". For a full exegesis of the theme, you are encouraged to refer to the book. However, this type of disunity is not deliberate, active division but insidious and passive indifference, which assumes that the work of ministry should only be left to pastors, preachers and other Christian leaders. Historically, most people did not go to school and therefore could not read or write and only theologians, priests and the bishops could. This meant that the work of preaching the gospel, teaching and making disciples became the sole preserve of a few elite and educated group of people, most of them male, who had to shoulder the burdens of ministry. Other people were left to carry out the menial tasks such as cleaning and cooking which of course are noble, but not the whole truth. The danger of overplaying such distinction is the tendency for certain men and women of God to fall into the trap of having special powers and unique revelation which only they could administer with no accountability, because of the unnecessary expectations church folk place on them. Great damage has been done to the name and testimony of Christ, including damaging families of certain ministers, because they spent too much time in church, and we need to resist this at all cost.

On the other extreme, we should be wary of leaders who are so insecure they feel they need to be involved with all aspects of church life from cooking, finances, budgeting and administration which is nothing but a controlling spirit. However, Acts 6:4 makes it very clear, the apostles gave themselves over to prayer and the preaching of the word. Of course it does not mean we don't know about these as we do have a certain level of accountability in some of these areas.

6. Gender division: women versus men

This is perhaps the most controversial but I believe an important discussion to have given the sometimes heated and polarised views that exist within the body of Christ in general and within certain denominations. This is particularly so in the area of church ministry and who qualifies for leadership. Of course, I don't intend to formulate a doctrine based on just one statement by Pharaoh; however, it will not be right to just gloss over it either. Pharaoh specifically and deliberately set out to separate men from women and men from children. If the church is so concerned about racial tensions and the generational divisions between the old and young, we must equally be concerned about the gender divisions between men and women both outside and within the church.

The fall of Adam and Eve in the garden brought significant divisions. One major consequence of the fall was the destruction of many relationships. Sin damaged relationships between:

- God and humanity;
- Man and woman (husband and wife);
- Parents and children;
- Cain and God;
- Cain and Abel.

We have touched on the case of Cain and Abel briefly in Chapter 4. Apart from the damage to the relationship between God and humanity, the next relation that suffered almost immediately, was marriage and the relationship between man (husband) and woman (wife) because the woman's desire became the man's. Unfortunately, this has always been interpreted to mean men can suppress and oppress women, but that does great injustice to the text. The truth is that God created both male and female in His image which meant they were equal in God's sight and both had different roles in fulfilling God's mandate for humanity in the earth. They were both blessed with the same blessing and both tasked with replenishing the earth. This worked fine until the serpent (devil) deceived Eve and then they started to accuse each other. I have a funny joke I always play on some of my friends, which is the fact that I do not believe in arranged marriages because of the fear of being blamed when things went wrong. Unfortunately, that is exactly what Adam did when God questioned him after he had eaten the forbidden fruit, instead of taking responsibility for his own actions. I believe this has not stopped and happens in marriages, in society and also within the church. Even men being head of the family can be stretched to mean dominance and dictatorship. It's quite interesting that people who insist on correct exegesis and hermeneutic interpretation of scripture take a scripture such as Ephesians 5:23 to relate to wedding ceremonies which is fine for application. However, Paul clearly states that he was talking about the mystery of Christ and His church before saying "nevertheless, let a man see to it that he loves his wife and the wife to submit. However, before he gave the specific instructions to men and women, he had clearly stated that everyone be submissive one to the other and later on that we love one another.

7. Forsaking the fellowship of other believers

This is particularly the case when we become only Sunday Christians with a touch and go mind-set without really being involved with the life of church and forming meaningful and fruitful relationships. I like Christian television very much but we must never use it as an excuse not to attend our local church unless we physically cannot. For example, when on a short trip where churches are remote. The writer to the Hebrews said clearly in chapter 10 verse 25, that "we should not forsake the assembling of ourselves together as is the manner of some". It is one of the key ways in which we grow and develop in our walk with God and to stay connected as part of the body. The early believers continued steadfastly not only in prayer and studying the bible but in daily fellowship. This goes beyond just 'normal' church activity but more importantly the fruit of living it out in friendships and supporting others outside formal church events.

It is important to give a caution here because after more than two decades of Christian ministry, I have come to the realisation that activities can replace real fellowship. Sometimes, there are too many church activities which do not in themselves foster fellowship and unity because people just bounce off each other. In certain extreme cases, church can become a basis to control people's lives, in that some parents feel obliged to spend more time in church than with their children and that is a dangerous imbalance which is another subtle form of Pharaoh's dividing bargain. Those of us who preach and in so called full time ministry, should never use the pulpit to diminish the importance of people's time spent with their families or even going to work. Both are equally as important as being in church because when families crumble and when people lose their jobs the church suffers. In addition, more pastoral time and effort has to be spent attending to these personal problems, instead of spending the time in spreading of the gospel. We must therefore be balanced and pragmatic in our approach to these things.

8. Classism and favouritism – James 2:1-13

I wish I was not writing about this or that it was not in the bible because it is the most difficult for Christians to admit, since everyone knows it is inherently wrong. However, it is in the bible and it did occur in church history. Further, because there is nothing new under the sun, I can bet my money that it does show up at least in our hearts once in a while. It is reported that Mahatma Gandhi read the gospels and became interested in Christian teaching, believing that Christianity could solve the caste system that divided Indians. But a steward in church refused him a seat, suggesting he worship with his own people. He left and never returned. "If Christians have caste differences also he said "I might as well remain a Hindu"[4, 5]. Prejudice and favouritism betrayed Jesus and turned a person away from trusting Him as Saviour. It is a scandal of historic proportions that some of the worst examples of discrimination and brutality have been committed under the guise of or with connivance of some Christians whether genuine or purported. These include the crusades, inquisition, slave trade, apartheid and the holocaust and in fact I have friends who have raised concerns about this tendency of Christianity and religion in general.

God is no respecter of persons, therefore no one should receive better treatment because of their economic, social or outward spiritual status. None of us will like to be called racist, so neither should we tolerate classism. God is the only judge over who comes into His kingdom and here another story will help. Susan Boyle the talented singer appeared on 'Britain's Got Talent' in 2008, with a non-celebrity appearance. Everyone expected a poor performance being crushed by a Simon Cowell insult. Then she opened her mouth and sang. The judges' eyes bulged, the crowd went silent. A writer for a weekly magazine, wrote this incredible confession: "In our pop-minded culture so obsessed with packaging - the right face, the right clothes, the right attitudes, the right Facebook posts - the unpackaged artistic power of the un-styled, Miss Boyle let me feel, for the duration of one blazing shows topping ballad, the meaning of human grace. She pierced my defences, reordered the measure of beauty. And I had no idea until tears sprang. How desperately I needed that corrective."

The church should be a place where everyone fits in and should not be a class or caste system. Of course I am aware that certain people can reach particular people groups more effectively and we should see that within the context of the beauty in diversity and not out of elitist separatism. So James advises us not to fall for this trick of Pharaoh but rather to be inclusive (James 2: 1 – 4).

The solution

I remember a strong piece of advice I was given by one of my mentors and tutors in bible school about unity. He said and I paraphrase, "... when you get out of here, make every effort to link up with other denominations irrespective of the differences in theology and non-essential beliefs, because God blesses unity". He was not saying this out of doctrinal correctness, because I know him to be a man of firm and strong biblical convictions. However, he was speaking out of several years of practical ministry experience. Here was someone who was raised as part of a movement that experienced the Pentecostal revival that arose in Wales and spent all his ministry life in a core Pentecostal denomination. However, he made such an impact in the Scottish highlands because in his own words, he was always willing to work with ministers from other denominations. He lived to experience the blessing that comes from unity of purpose. Of course he did not believe in uniformity and held onto to his core beliefs but was able to work alongside people he even disagreed with so together, they powerfully testified of Jesus Christ to fulfil His Great commission which should be our first concern. Bishop T.D. Jakes during the opening of one of his pastors and leadership conferences put it this way, "to be an effective leader, you must learn to cross pollinate". In other words, it is vital to intermingle with people of different persuasions to ours if we are going to make meaningful impact in our very diverse and complex world. The idea that we have it all and that we are the only custodians of God's revelation and calling, is not only fanciful, but quite frankly, arrogance towards God, as both Jesus and Moses related to the disciples and Joshua respectively. That is why Moses and Aaron were having none of Pharaoh's tricks and neither should we.

Before we complete this long chapter, it is important to remember the scripture in Psalm 133 which was quoted at the very beginning.

"How **good** and **pleasant** it is when **brothers live together in unity**! It is like **precious oil** poured on the head, running down on the beard, running down on Aaron's beard, down upon the collar of his robes. It is as if the **dew of Hermon** were falling on **Mount Zion**. For there the LORD bestows his blessing, even life forevermore".

One commentator[6] has described Psalm 133 this way and I quote "the Psalm is a perfect picture of unity - **a divine unity**: the sharing of the blessings of God, poured out in love upon us all. How foolish to suppose that biblical fellowship can be enjoyed by those who do not share the blessing of a common hope! But how foolish also to suppose that God views favourably any division among those who, despite minor differences, do share a common hope".

"In summary, this Psalm forms part of the long series of songs referred to as "songs of degrees" or "songs of ascents" beginning from Psalm 110, representing the songs the Israelites sang as they undertook their pilgrimage up the hill towards the temple on mount Zion to worship. Its ultimate aim is unity of worship and communion, with God at the centre, and not the individual or a denomination. It is corporate worship at its best, and the only thing God will bless. And so we find the expression of our unity in the **ascending** of our common petitions and the **descending** of our common blessings. True brothers of Christ are united in one hope, one need, and one experience".

Unfortunately, the word blessing has become a dirty word in certain Christian circles which is quite troubling because it runs through the bible right from creation, through Abraham, Isaac and Jacob and eventually in Christ. We have opted for the safe 'gospel of negativity' because of a spirit of religion, which is not found in scripture. The blessing was so important, Esau was prepared to kill Jacob who stole his birth right, even though he had no physical evidence of this blessing. It was so important, Jacob sought it out with all his energy in his struggle with the angel of God till his name (deceiver) was changed to Israel (prince with God). Another commentator has described Psalm 133 as the "descent of divine blessing"[7] depicted by the oil on Aaron's head and dew of Hermon. In the King James Version, three verbs precede the words used to represent the flow of unity which triggers the flow of God's blessing as they ascend in unity to the place of united worship, centred on God Himself. These are "ran down", "went down" and "descended". In the NIV, the phrases are "running down", "down" and "falling on". In the Greek, the same word is used which is translated "descended". Unity with Christ is intimately bound up with unity with our brethren which is not only good but also pleasant. We cannot have one without the other. When we recognise this unity, then God commands the blessing.

The role of leadership
If we are honest, leadership has been the source of more disunity in the body of Christ than its members have been. Leaders in local churches and maybe within denominations may be good at having a semblance of unity within their ranks but viciously promote disunity based on doctrine, style (songs, preaching and liturgy) and personality which is quite hypocritical. The fact that a leader does not like another leader is not enough grounds to transfer that to the whole congregation. Even in cases of doctrinal error, we should temper it with grace and love. Within local churches and some denominations,

it is not uncommon to find primary leaders practicing the dangerous secular trait of divide and rule which is a controlling spirit that we should resist at all cost. To put it bluntly, we must refuse to submit to such an attitude as it is very ungodly and quite frankly, carnal.

James describes two types of wisdom in the famous chapter about the dangers and blessings of the tongue and makes this strong statement.

"Who is wise and understanding among you? Let him show it by his good life, by deeds done in the humility that comes from wisdom. But if you harbour bitter envy and selfish ambition in your hearts, do not boast about it or deny the truth. Such "wisdom" does not come down from heaven but is earthly, unspiritual, of the devil. For where you have envy and selfish ambition, there you find disorder and every evil practice. But the wisdom that comes from heaven is first of all pure; then peace-loving, considerate, submissive, full of mercy and good fruit, impartial and sincere. Peacemakers who sow in peace raise a harvest of righteousness".

James 3:13-18

Ephesians Chapter 4 and the role of leadership

God indeed blesses unity and of course the devil can only do the opposite, which is undermining unity in all its forms and facets. We need to resist it whilst standing for the things which we believe to be non-negotiable and therefore not compromise. In Ephesians chapter 4, we have probably the most important chapter spelling out the people who make up the primary leadership of any church and what their key functions are. The book of Ephesians is in my opinion one of Paul's master pieces and unsurprisingly, we are described as "God's masterpiece" in Ephesians 3 verse 10. The book is split into three main sections

Chapters 1 - 3	Wealth of the Believer	or	Calling	of the Believer
Chapters 4 - 6 v 9	Walk of the Believer	or	Conduct	of the Believer
Chapter 6: v 10 - 20	Warfare of the Believer	or	Conflict	of the Believer

Chapter 4 deals with walking in unity and in love. How does this come about? Well the answer is right in the chapter because from the outset, Paul sets out clearly his desire that we make every effort to keep the unity of the Spirit in the bond of peace. Then he goes on to give us reasons why this is important because:

(i)   we are **one** body,
(ii)   there is **one** Spirit,
(iii)   we are called to **one** hope,
(iv)   there is **one** Lord,
(v)   we have **one** faith,
(vi)   we experience **one** baptism,
(vii)   we have come to **one** God and Father of all.

Interestingly, the God-head (Father, Son and Holy Spirit) who are the perfect representation of unity are all listed here. However, this unity does not rest in a vacuum but has much diversity because there are different individuals and varieties of gifts. You can experience this unity in diversity and not in uniformity. This is where the role of leadership comes in (Ephesians 4: 11 - 12). The goal of the chapter is that we all come to the unity of the faith and of the knowledge of Jesus Christ, and by what everyone contributes, we grow and are built together in love (Ephesians 4: 13 - 16). There will always be differences of some sort, a lot of it due to our carnal inclinations but we must always keep Christ central in all we do, and that will help us overcome this trap of the enemy. In the next chapter, we will deal with a tricky bargain of money and material resources as presented by Pharaoh, which is in itself a source of disunity in the church and society in general.

CHAPTER 7 CASH BARGAIN – RELIGIOUS WORSHIP
(Giving and Resourcing the Kingdom)
(Exodus 10:24 – 26)

"This is the miracle that happens every time to those who really love; the more they give, the more they possess".

Rainer Maria Rilke

"Give a man a fish and you feed him for a day. Teach him to fish and you feed him for a lifetime"

Chinese Proverb

We have so far deliberated extensively upon four tricks which the enemy of our souls has employed throughout the ages against our spiritual walk. Unable to overcome Moses' persistence, tenacity and unwavering refusal to compromise, Pharaoh finally goes for the unexpected trap which most religious people easily fall into, because somehow money is tantamount to evil. I am referring to the debate about material things captured under the word 'money' and whether it has a place in Christian life. Pharaoh said, "leave all your substance and go have good spiritual worship and sacrifice". However, there could be no sacrifice and complete worship without the goats and sheep which definitely cost money. Before we dig deeper into this controversial but important subject, let's note the following:

> a. It is very easy in popular religion to paint material things as evil, even when we blatantly enjoy them in the name of a minimum standard of living in an affluent country. Picture the scenario of a man who buys a new and expensive brand of car for himself and gives his used but beautiful one to a family member and yet spends all his time criticising another Christian who owns a jet because somehow, to him, the jet is too expensive. Now I do not own a jet and I'm perfectly happy to fly economy class during my regular overseas travels. The problem I have with such reasoning is that whilst a jet is definitely expensive, it is also obvious that the

particular brand of car is equally expensive compared to what the average person drives and to others who have to commute on the bus every day. However, I refuse to condemn both this individual and the one with the jet because it is not my money, especially if they have not stolen or exploited others.

b. You are considered more spiritual when you leave your work, sometimes out of blackmail, to go into so called 'full time' as if God is not interested in our work.

c. Some people say their daily job is 'secular employment' and church activity is 'ministry' to God. This is one of the biggest lies ever perpetuated among Christians because we forget that God will hold us to account on both fronts. Such thinking also makes the church lose credibility with the world and make us appear out of touch.

d. Money is wrongly (and falsely) called the 'root of all evil' when the bible laid the blame with the individual person, that is; "the love of money is the root of all evil". Money cannot love money, so money cannot be the root of evil. People quote Matthew 6 verse 24 which says "no man can serve God and money" yet forget that we can actually serve God with our money. This is the solution to the dangerous trait of loving money, through giving in the form of tithes, offerings, to charity, helping the poor, family members and other believers in need.

e. Some people think tithes belong to the law and the Old Testament and therefore have no place in the New Testament Church. However, tithes were instituted before the law was given, during a dispensation of God's covenant with Abraham, which was a covenant based on faith. The giving of tithes and offerings honour God and is a sign of real commitment to Him. This is because money represents our life, time and toil and where our treasure is, there our heart will be also (Proverbs 3:9-10).

Pharaoh's age old trick

Now let's revisit Pharaoh's last and probably the most dangerous of his bargains because it is the easiest to fall for and unfortunately is common in Christian circles these days.

"Then Pharaoh summoned Moses and said, go, worship the LORD. Even your women and children may go with you; **only leave your flocks and herds behind.** But Moses said, you must **allow us to have sacrifices and burnt offerings to present to the LORD our God. Our livestock too must go with us; not a hoof is to be left behind. We have to use some of them in worshipping the LORD our God, and until we get there we will not know what we are to use to worship the LORD"**

Exodus 10: 22 - 24

Before we expand on this exciting and interesting portion of the bible, I can almost anticipate people's protest with other bible quotes such as "offering our bodies as living sacrifices, holy and acceptable to God", as found in Romans 12. Of course this is true, but here is the problem; Pharaoh clearly suggests that all of such is fine as long as we keep worshipping in an unbalanced way. He is even happy for them to remain united in their worship because whilst previously he wanted only the men to go, he now says even the women and children can go with you to worship as long as you have nothing to worship with.

By insisting they leave their flocks and herds behind, Pharaoh was implying that everything they'd worked for and acquired was not important in their worship of God and not part of their story of freedom and deliverance. However, that could not be further from the truth, because when Jacob led his family into Egypt at the invitation of Joseph, they came with the men, women, children and also their flocks and cattle. Some of these herds will have been used to carry loads and luggage including possibly the children and weaker members, so it made perfect sense to be going back with these and the ones acquired in Egypt.

Besides, their history right from the time of Abel, Abraham, Isaac and Jacob was littered with examples of offering sacrifices to God as part of their worship as well as being a sign of their commitment to God and of their covenant relationship with Him. It was their source of livelihood including the tilling of the ground, which was mandated by God right from creation, so this was a real attempt to disempower them both economically and also psychologically.

Perhaps, a more recent illustration will be helpful here. Around the late 1940s, 1950s and early 1960s, most nations under colonial rule, including my native Ghana started agitating for independence and self-rule from colonial masters. After several years of struggle, independence was granted but as most commentators agree, this was largely just political with little economic independence. The long history of slavery and looting of these countries' wealth and human resources meant economic and psychological dependence which was no independence at all. As we speak, most of these countries are dependent on international foreign aid to survive, let alone live comfortably. A lot of these countries are saddled with excessive debt to their former Colonial masters, the World Bank and the International Monetary Fund, which means they remain at the mercy of these countries and institutions in terms of their own policy decisions. Of course, a lot of problems in developing countries can also be attributed to corruption and poor leadership, which needs to be said bluntly, but we cannot deny the damage that economic dependency has done to the 'developing world' psyche. The result has been deprivation, disease, wars and conflicts some of which are still being fought today.

This is brilliantly captured by my senior colleague from secondary school, Caleb Ayiku[8] on his Facebook post of 25 May 2015, in celebration of African Union (AU) Day.

"More than a generation ago our leaders gathered to establish the OAU. Those leaders were united in the quest for political emancipation of the continent. They achieved their aim. What they did not realize was that the colonialist never left Africa. Africa is under economic oppression. Question: What are we going to do about it? No people ever liberated themselves without a struggle. To leave the Egypt of economic oppression we have to fight a few battles. There may be casualties. We may have to endure some pain and some hardship. The truth is that the current construct of AU will not liberate Africa. The current crop of leaders are either asleep or have been blinded by the colonialist. Our generation must produce new African leaders across the land. In Ghana and in Nigeria. In Kenya and in Burundi. In Mali and DRC we need leaders of like mind. Like Patrice, Nyerere and Nkrumah who stood for political emancipation, a new breed of 5 or 6 or 7 leaders have to emerge to stand for economic liberation of our continent. Individual countries cannot end the oppression. To defeat the oppressor we need a number of like-minded leaders in a union. Just like we need a critical mass of leaders at various levels across sectors to build our nation. Our generation must do something for the quality of life we crave for our continent. I shudder to think about the continent our children will live in. ...." "We need Christian leaders who will obey God's voice in their leadership. So pray for the AU. And pray for Ghana that our current leaders find their way".

Caleb Ayiku, Public Figure

It is the same trick Pharaoh played with Moses and God's people which we must always reject. In the church, the story is not much different. There are people who will vehemently defend their hatred of money because they see it as a force for evil and yet spend lots of efforts 'begging' for money to be given to them for missions in poorer countries. My pointed question will be, will it not be great if the Christians in these poorer countries had enough resources to be able to support the work of God in their own countries and surrounding needy neighbours? In fact, this economic dependency can sometimes be used as leverage to influence vision and mission in such places. Of course, we do not want to take this too far as I believe firmly that these efforts are genuine. However, my conviction is that it's always better to empower people by providing capacity building, which is captured by the following Chinese proverb:

"Give a man a fish and you feed him for a day. Teach him to fish and you feed him for a lifetime"

Therefore, whilst it is good to give a hungry man some fish, it is far better to teach them how to fish, so they can fend not only for themselves but for their families and other people in need. That is a well-known economic fact and the most effective aid these days come in the form of capacity building involving more training and equipping rather than just spoon feeding. Such spoon feeding has created the dependency syndrome we see all over Africa and much of Asia where whole economies depend on foreign aid. That goes against normal human dignity and the church should not in any way be overtly supporting this tendency by spiritualising the whole debate about money and in some extreme cases, demonising it. Such thinking is definitely falling into a dangerous trap, as Pharaoh tried to set for Moses. Of course we should not love money and it should not control us and we will address some of dangers with loving money and how to avoid falling into that trap later in this chapter.

Moses' response

As noted earlier, we cannot serve God and money, but we can definitely serve God with our money and material resources. This is exactly how Moses responded to Pharaoh. We will need all our possessions in order to serve God and we cannot categorise certain things as non-spiritual when we don't know when God will require them as part of our worship. How can we feed the hungry, homeless and vulnerable in society if we promote a poverty mind set in the name of spirituality? The church has done amazing things in the areas of medicine, nursing, education, justice and human rights, sanitation and social care and none of these could be done without money or the material and human resources whose training required money. In scientific research, a lot of the current neglected diseases including malaria and leishmaniasis are funded by rich philanthropists such as Bill Gates and yet a lot of these billionaires are agnostics or atheists, though a few are religious. The big question is, where are the Christians? It's not enough in my opinion to just look after people when they have fallen ill or support them to have a dignified death, I am in favour of all of that. But my goodness, as a researcher and health professional, investing money and resources to both prevent and cure these dreadful diseases is better than the former. There is nothing spiritual in my opinion, in seeing people suffer needless diseases when these can be easily cured with the needed financial resource. How can children and pregnant mothers in the 21st century still die of malaria and the church is silent about that, though we scream about other ills in society?

However, there are lots of positives, because I believe the church is still a force for good. Some of my favourite institutions include the Oral Roberts University and World Vision who have done amazing things with God's help in equipping and empowering churches and communities in the developing world including providing free health care. These things which are valid ministry outreaches cost money and I believe God will reward them abundantly at the Judgment seat of Christ. In a recent study, dubbed the Faith Action Audit, undertaken by a social action group, Cinnamon Network and published on 21 May 2015, it was discovered that faith groups including Christians, Jews, Muslims and other religious bodies, contributed more than £3 billion a year in social action to UK communities.

The fact that it is provided free does not mean no one had to pay for it and those who paid for it could not do it if they had no money. However, we do need to apply a lot of wisdom in our dealings with money so it can be maximised and used for the glory of God. That is why Solomon said the following in Ecclesiastes:

"Wisdom, like an inheritance, is a good thing and benefits those who see the sun. Wisdom is a shelter as money is a shelter, but the advantage of knowledge is this: Wisdom preserves those who have it."

Ecclesiastes 7: 11 – 12 (KJV)

"By much slothfulness the building decays; and through idleness of the hands the house drops through. A feast is made for laughter, and wine makes merry: but money answers all things."

Ecclesiastes 10:18 – 19 (KJV)

God's validation
To show the importance of this theme and how seriously God viewed it, He asked the children of Israel not just to leave Egypt with their flocks and herds but to ask for gold and jewels from the Egyptians in Exodus chapter 11. A covenant people always have a material element to their blessing and we are in grave error when we try to separate the two. This temptation is what has led to the double life of many believers because we lead compartmentalised lives

between church, family, business, career and our social pursuits. Abraham never backslid because of his material blessings, neither did Isaac, Jacob or Joseph. All their troubles had to do with character, and yet any mention of financial or material blessing sounds like the devil himself has come to town, which is quite troubling. Some Christian leaders will condemn another preacher living in luxury and yet find nothing wrong with spending money on ventures God never asked them to pursue in the first place.

The cure for love of money (1 Timothy chapter 6; 2 Corinthians chapter 9)

All of the above notwithstanding, it is also vital to bring some balance to this discussion and it will be intellectually and theologically dishonest to avoid it. This is because Paul warned about the lust of the eyes, the love of money and the strong temptation to serve God just for money (or filthy lucre). That always leads to disaster which must also be avoided at all cost. A typical example is the credit card craze and most of us, including churches, living beyond our means in order to 'keep up with the Jones'. That is ungodly and we need to repent from such excesses. Neither should people be blackmailed into giving money which they do not have. However, since this is not the major aim of this chapter, let us now turn our attention to a few practical examples of how to serve God with our money and material things as listed below:

1. First of all offer your body as a living sacrifice, holy and acceptable to God which is our reasonable spiritual worship.
2. Use your gifts, talents, expertise, training and work experience. For example Oral Roberts University Medical Team, World Vision, Medicine San Frontier, Mission Aviation Fellowship, Operation Mobilisation all employ highly skilled Christian workers to be the hands and feet of Christ to meet human needs all of which cost money.
3. Give money towards missions, church vision and church plants, particularly in very remote places.
4. Your home can be a place for small group bible study and a lot of good churches started that way.
5. What about technology? Some people say it's the world come into the church. However, God gave man the inherent capacity to rule, subdue and replenish the earth. The rejection

of God by certain scientists does not mean whatever man produces is evil. I believe that in reality, we mainly discover what God has created. Science is based primarily on natural laws which I believe could only have been set in motion by God, the creator of the universe and the one who set the boundaries for the seas. This may sound surprising, but do you know that Jesus could come back today because the one sign among others that precedes His return, could potentially be fulfilled within a short time? Jesus said, "this gospel of the kingdom will be preached in all nations of the earth then the earth will come". He did not mention the medium and did not restrict it to missionaries and church planters. He did not even say everyone will be saved. Therefore, we could be waiting for revival when God is preparing to come back. Modern technologies including mobile phones, the internet, email, satellite television, Facebook, Twitter, Instagram, WhatsApp, Viber, Skype, video messaging means the gospel can now reach closed countries more easily. We don't necessarily have to risk smuggling bibles to such places anymore. Paul said we must be wise and make use of every opportunity.

6. Give generously to the poor and the needy: This last point is probably the best cure to the love of money in the midst of our abundance.

In his daily bible devotion on 2 Corinthians chapter 9 verses 6-15, for 7 September 2014, as part of the popular Bible In One Year (BIOY), Nicky Gumbel[9], Vicar of Holy Trinity Brompton in London, outlines the following 10 reasons for giving generously and these are reproduced in full below.

1. **It is the best investment you can make**
   Like the harvest, giving is planting seed. The farmer will reap far more than what was sown (v.6): 'A stingy planter gets a stingy crop; a lavish planter gets a lavish crop' (v.6, MSG). This applies to everything in life. What you give to the Lord he multiplies – your time, gifts, ambitions and money.

2. **It should be fun**

   Giving should never be forced or grudging, but rather voluntary and cheerful. 'Let each one give as he has made up his own mind and purposed in his heart, not reluctantly or sorrowfully or under compulsion, for God loves (He takes pleasure in, prizes above all other things, and is unwilling to abandon or to do without) a cheerful (joyous, "prompt to do it") giver whose heart is in his giving' (v.7, AMP). The Greek word for cheerful is hilaros and our giving should be hilarious! It should be fun to give.

3. **It takes away the burden of financial worry**

   Paul writes, 'and God is able to make all grace abound to you, so that in all things at all times, having all that you need, you will abound in every good work' (v.8). Giving does not mean handing over financial responsibility to God – but it does mean handing over the worry and the burden of it.

4. **It 'enriches' you**

   When God invites us to give, he is pleading to our reason, not to our emotions: 'Thus you will be enriched in all things and in every way so that you can be generous' (v.11, AMP). Materially, we will have enough to give away generously (v.11). Our characters will be enriched (v.10). God will be praised (v.11).

5. **It transforms your character**

   Paul speaks of 'the harvest of your righteousness' (v.10b). Giving purges the character from the constricting grip of materialism that destroys lives.

6. **It inspires others**

   'Your generosity will result in thanksgiving to God. This service that you perform is not only supplying the needs of God's people but it is also overflowing in the many expressions of thanks to God. Because of the service of which you approved yourselves, people will praise God' (vv.11b–13a).

7. **It meets people's needs**

   Generous giving blesses other people and supplies the needs of God's people – 'helping meet the bare needs of poor Christians' (v.12, MSG).

8. **It is evidence of real faith**
   Generous giving is an act of obedience, which should accompany 'your confession of the gospel of Christ' (v.13). Giving is an act of trust – in doing it we are saying that it is God, not ourselves or anyone else, who ultimately provides for our needs.

9. **It makes you a stakeholder in the church**
   Paul speaks of 'your generosity in sharing with them and with everyone else' (v.13b). The word Paul uses for sharing is koinonia which can also be translated 'fellowship'. In the same way as when you share a flat or apartment you share in the bills, as you share in the needs of the community you reap the benefits of that community. For example, every time someone comes to know Christ through the community you share in the blessing.

10. **It is a response to God's gift to you**
    Our giving is a response to God's amazing grace. His 'indescribable gift' (v.15) is the gift of his Son. 'Thank God for this gift, his gift. No language can praise it enough!' (v.15, MSG).

The Local Church Application
We have talked about the dangers of dependency, which is probably the game Pharaoh was playing. In the same way that the men will have had to come back regularly to Egypt if their women and children had stayed behind, it is possible, they will have always felt the need to go back to Egypt to have their material needs met. Even after all the miraculous demonstrations, the smallest scent of trouble and challenges were enough to trigger this tendency of desiring to go back to Egypt to eat cucumbers and onions.

Therefore what does this mean for the church, in particular at a community and local level? What are some of the ideal models and lessons we can learn from this principle? Well, there is no better place than the bible. Let's turn to the early church in the book of Acts right after Pentecost and the coming of the Holy Spirit for some clues and important principles on this subject.

"They devoted themselves to the apostles' teaching and to fellowship, to the breaking of bread and to prayer. Everyone was filled with awe at the many wonders and signs performed by the apostles. All the believers were together and had everything in common. They sold property and possessions to give to anyone who had need. Every day they continued to meet together in the temple courts. They broke bread in their homes and ate together with glad and sincere hearts, praising God and enjoying the favour of all the people. And the Lord added to their number daily those who were being saved."

Acts 2: 42 – 47

All the believers were one in heart and mind. No one claimed that any of their possessions was their own, but they shared everything they had. With great power the apostles continued to testify to the resurrection of the Lord Jesus. And God's grace was so powerfully at work in them all that there were no needy persons among them. For from time to time those who owned land or houses sold them, brought the money from the sales and put it at the apostles' feet, and it was distributed to anyone who had need. Joseph, a Levite from Cyprus, whom the apostles called Barnabas (which means son of encouragement), sold a field he owned and brought the money and put it at the apostles' feet.

Acts 4: 32 - 37

In summary, for any church movement and local church to be successful and make meaningful impact, they need to be:

Self-governing – Good local leadership and ministries

Self-sustaining – Sound human resources to do the work of ministry

Self-propagating – With the above two, they are able to pursue the primary calling of every church which is propagating the message and gospel of the kingdom of Jesus Christ.

Self-supporting – All the above vital elements of local church, are in part dependent on being able to resource these financially and materially through training, church programmes, meeting individual and community needs, supporting the poor and investing in new ministries, all of which cost money. This must happen both at the corporate and individual levels as happened in Acts chapters two, four and five.

Financing the gospel in the face of secular propaganda
The Resurrection Story

After the Sabbath, at dawn on the first day of the week, Mary Magdalene and the other Mary went to look at the tomb. There was a violent earthquake, for an angel of the Lord came down from heaven and, going to the tomb, rolled back the stone and sat on it. His appearance was like lightning, and his clothes were white as snow. **The guards were so afraid of him that they shook and became like dead men.** The angel said to the women, do not be afraid, for I know that you are looking for Jesus, who was crucified. He is not here; he has risen, just as he said. Come and see the place where he lay. Then go quickly and tell his disciples: 'He has risen from the dead and is going ahead of you into Galilee. There you will see him. Now I have told you. So the women hurried away from the tomb, afraid yet filled with joy, and ran to tell his disciples. Suddenly Jesus met them. Greetings, he said. They came to him, clasped his feet and worshiped him. Then Jesus said to them, do not be afraid. Go and tell my brothers to go to Galilee; there they will see me. **While the women were on their way, some of the guards went into the city and reported to the chief priests everything that had happened.** When the chief priests had met with the elders and devised a plan, **they gave the soldiers a large sum of money, telling them,** you are to say, His disciples came during the night and stole him away while we were asleep. If this report gets to the governor, we will satisfy him and keep you out of trouble. **So the soldiers took the money and did as they were instructed. And this story has been widely circulated among the Jews to this very day."**

Matthews 28: 1 -15

This is probably the most important story in the bible because the message of the gospel is incomplete without the resurrection of Jesus Christ from the dead. Paul stated strongly, that if Christ is not risen from the dead, then we are of all men the most miserable (1 Corinthians 15: 19). Here were the Roman guards who by all accounts were among the first to witness directly the events surrounding the resurrection of Jesus. You will have thought that such an encounter will provoke them to believing first of all and then subsequently become witnesses of the resurrection. However, the scripture says, whilst Mary and the disciples were on their way to announce this headline story, the soldiers went to tell the Chief Priests. This is quite interesting but also very unusual, as soldiers will normally be expected to report such an important matter first to their commander. In the US, the President who is Commander-In-Chief of the armed forces is briefed on anything important to national security and the keeping of the peace. It is therefore very surprising that these soldiers did not pass on this information up the chain of command and possibly eventually, to Pilate himself. This is where things get interesting but serious, within the context of this chapter.

You may be asking, what has this got to do with the resurrection story? Well, in the same way Pharaoh wanted to prevent the children of Israel from taking their substance to worship God with, Roman soldiers, who were the best trained and most disciplined military of the day, were not only bribed into silence with money, but also to actively propagate a falsehood that persisted right down till the writing of the book of Matthew and I believe still persists today. How common is it to find some of the richest people in the world, including celebrities, espousing and bankrolling some of the most anti-Christian messages currently propagated around the world? If money can allow falsehood against the message of the gospel, then in a more positive sense, the opposite can also true. Money and material things, dedicated to God's cause, can and will help propagate the truth of the gospel, as discussed below from Luke.

Supporters of Jesus' Ministry

"After this, Jesus travelled about from one town and village to another, proclaiming the good news of the kingdom of God. The Twelve were with him, and also some women who had been cured of evil spirits and diseases: Mary (called Magdalene) from whom seven demons had come out; Joanna the wife of Chuza, the manager of Herod's household; Susanna; and many others. **These women were helping to support them out of their own means**."

Luke 8:1 – 3

These women supported Jesus and His disciples from their own resources, not begging for charitable donations. These precious women ministered to Jesus not through evangelism, singing, cleaning the church but out of their substance. It is interesting that the parable of the sower follows immediately after this short statement about their ministry. Trying to squeeze money out of all conversations about ministry is not only a grave mistake but quite dangerous.

Now let's go deeper because Luke chapter 8 verse 1 says "after these things", referring clearly to what had just gone on previously. Therefore, to understand this context properly, it is important to refer to that and I have reproduced the relevant verses below, from the Message Bible.

"One of the Pharisees asked him over for a meal. He went to the Pharisee's house and sat down at the dinner table. Just then a woman of the village, the town harlot, having learned that Jesus was a guest in the home of the Pharisee, came with a bottle of very expensive perfume and stood at his feet, weeping, raining tears on his feet. Letting down her hair, she dried his feet, kissed them, and anointed them with the perfume. When the Pharisee who had invited him saw this, he said to himself, If this man was the prophet I thought he was, he would have known what kind of woman this is who is falling all over him. Jesus said to him, Simon, I have something to tell you. Oh? Tell me. Two men were in debt to a banker. One owed five hundred silver pieces, the other fifty. Neither of them could pay up, and so the banker cancelled both debts. Which of the two would be more grateful? Simon answered, I suppose the one who was forgiven the most. That's right, said Jesus. Then turning to the woman, but speaking to Simon, he said, do you see this woman? I came to your home; you provided no water for my feet, but she rained tears on my feet and dried them with her hair. You gave me no greeting, but from the time I arrived she hasn't quit kissing my feet. You provided nothing for freshening up, but she has soothed my feet with perfume. Impressive, isn't it? She was forgiven many, many sins, and so she is very, very grateful. If the forgiveness is minimal, the gratitude is minimal. Then he spoke to her: I forgive your sins. That set the dinner guests talking behind his back: Who does he think he is, forgiving sins! He ignored them and said to the woman, "Your faith has saved you. Go in peace."

Luke 7: 36 - 50

It is quite obvious that one of these so called sinful women, possibly

Mary Magdalene, was part of the group supporting Jesus out of their own resources. Interestingly, in the other gospels where this story is told, Judas Iscariot complained about this woman wasting the oil she anointed Jesus Christ with. We must resist the urge to glorify and sanctify lack and poverty whilst at the same time maintaining the moral high ground to be able to challenge a market and capitalist culture driven by greed, covetousness and materialism which has resulted in excessive exploitation of the poor by the rich and powerful at the personal, social, national and international level. Our lust for things we don't need and cannot afford, has led to excessive amounts of national and household debts which we must repent from. The credit crunch and financial banking crisis of 2008 is still fresh in our memories, with countries such as Greece still reeling from its lingering effects.

The church and the secular government
There is a current arrangement, between most charitable organisations, of which the church is a part, as far as money is concerned which I want to briefly consider within the context of this chapter. The church like all other religious groupings is considered a non-profit organisation and therefore largely exempt from taxes such as corporation tax. Of course this does not include business spin off activities run by the church for profit, where fair tax contributions are expected. The tax exempt arrangements vary from country to country with some being more generous than others. In the UK for example, the scheme is very generous because, not only is the church exempt from corporation tax, but the government also donates up to 25% for each pound donated to the charity by eligible UK tax payers. This is formally referred to as 'gift aid' and as a former church trustee I know how vital it is to budgets and the smooth running of many churches and other charitable organisations. In the US, this exempt arrangement is set out in federal tax law[10] and among other things prohibits churches from engaging in direct partisan politics where churches endorse one party or its candidate over the other. The law does provide some balance when it comes to ministers who speak and write and advise them to always state that they speak in their own personal capacity. I have taken the following paragraph from the document referenced above:

"The political campaign activity prohibition is not intended to restrict free expression on political matters by leaders of churches or religious organizations speaking for themselves, as individuals. Nor are leaders prohibited from speaking about important issues of public policy. **However, for their organizations to remain tax exempt under IRC section 501(c)(3), religious leaders cannot make partisan comments in official organization publications or at official church functions.** To avoid potential attribution of their comments outside of church functions and publications, religious leaders who speak or write in their individual capacity are encouraged to clearly indicate that their comments are personal and not intended to represent the views of the organization."

Personally, I believe, that some of these political boundaries are sensible if kept narrow as was originally intended. This is because politics by its nature is a very divisive enterprise and churches, whilst keeping their right to speak on social issues and policy which affect their members, should be careful not to divide the church and its members along political party lines. Unfortunately, this is as far as things go, because this tax exempt status and pecks such as gift aid, have sometimes been used in a stick and carrot fashion, to beat up the church, when governments have felt 'threatened' by churches' stance on certain public policies. This is where the principle we've learnt about Pharaoh's tricks become vital. Money is a very powerful tool, which some in the church unfortunately treat as evil and yet we have no qualms fighting tooth and nail to keep our tax exempt status. In fact, it is probably safe to say so many churches in the UK for example, may not be able to balance their books without gift aid rebates from the government. It is very easy for such non-binding support from government to be used as a blackmail and manipulative tool to force the church into a culture of silence where we cannot easily comment on the excesses of government and wrong immoral policies.

My personal view, is that churches should put in place sound financial planning, including investments, with appropriate and reliable returns to keep the machinery of church going, in the event of such pecks being withdrawn or significantly reduced. I believe this is biblical because in the bible, the source of money for the temple and its running as well as in the New Testament, was contributions from the children of Israel. This is clearly the case later in Exodus, when people gave towards the building of the tabernacle, so much so that, Moses had to beg them to stop giving.

"The LORD said to Moses, tell the Israelites to bring me an offering. You are to receive the offering for me from everyone whose heart prompts them to give. These are the offerings you are to receive from them: gold, silver and bronze; blue, purple and scarlet yarn and fine linen; goat hair; ram skins dyed red and another type of durable leather; acacia wood; olive oil for the light; spices for the anointing oil and for the fragrant incense; and onyx stones and other gems to be mounted on the ephod and breast piece. Then have them make a sanctuary for me, and I will dwell among them. Make this tabernacle and all its furnishings exactly like the pattern I will show you."

Exodus 25: 1 – 9

"Then the LORD said to Moses, See, I have chosen Bezalel son of Uri, the son of Hur, of the tribe of Judah, and I have filled him with the Spirit of God, with wisdom, with understanding, with knowledge and with all kinds of skills—to make artistic designs for work in gold, silver and bronze, to cut and set stones, to work in wood, and to engage in all kinds of crafts. Moreover, I have appointed Oholiab son of Ahisamak, of the tribe of Dan, to help him. Also I have given ability to all the skilled workers to make everything I have commanded you: the tent of meeting, the ark of the covenant law with the atonement cover on it, and all the other furnishings of the tent - the table and its articles, the pure gold lampstand and all its accessories, the altar of incense, the altar of burnt offering and all its utensils, the basin with its stand— and also the woven garments, both the sacred garments for Aaron the priest and the garments for his sons when they serve as priests, and the anointing oil and fragrant incense for the Holy Place."

Exodus 31: 1 - 11

That is the principle of more than enough, instead of the tendency in church to just budget for what I call hand to mouth living, where we're literally living on the breadline and any massive shock, such as a sudden withdrawal of aid, or a regular donor leaving could tip us over the edge. The fear of money (which is genuine) by most believers is so pervasive, it can even lead to misquoting and misinterpretation of certain portions of scripture. I believe we must depend on the Holy Spirit based on the finished work of Christ. However, I have a way of coping and dealing with this real danger which I want us to explore very briefly, and hopefully it helps you as well. Most people quote the famous verse by Jesus as he preached the 'sermon on the mount'

"No one can serve two masters, for you will either love one or hate the other..... You cannot serve God and money".

Matthew 6:24

That is absolutely true, but unfortunately most of us have misrepresented the last part of this verse. It never said you cannot have money as Pharaoh tried to do. Neither did it say money was evil. Of course this section formed part of His 'sermon on the mount' series or the beatitudes which talk about values and principles in Christ's new kingdom. These principles are different to the way the secular and I dare say, the religious systems operate. This part of the sermon deals with priorities, which culminates in another famous verse in the series found in Matthew 6:33, "seek ye first the kingdom and His righteousness......" So how do we avoid the impossible task of serving God and money which really amounts to serving money? The answer I believe **is to serve God with our money**, the same way we present our bodies as living sacrifices unto God, which is the same thing Moses insisted upon.

Conclusion
To finish off, I'll like to end with this quote by Rainer Maria Rilke: "This is the miracle that happens every time to those who really love; the more they give, the more they possess". No wonder Paul could say, "as having nothing, yet we possess all things, as poor yet making many rich" (2 Corinthians 6 vs 10).

CHAPTER 8 COMPLETE BARGAIN – TRUE SPIRITUAL WORSHIP
(The Real Deal - Exodus 12:31-32)

"Almighty God, you have made us for yourself, and our hearts are restless till they find their rest in you; so lead us by your Spirit that in this life we may live to your glory and in the life to come enjoy you forever; through Jesus Christ our Lord who is alive with you and the Holy Spirit, one God now and forever".

St Augustine Confessions

"The core of the person is what he or she loves, and that is bound up with what they worship - that insight recalibrates the radar for cultural analysis. The rituals and practices that form our loves spill out well beyond the sanctuary. Many secular liturgies are trying to get us to love some other kingdom and some other gods".

Dallas Willard

"Pharaoh rose up in the night, he, all his servants, and all the Egyptians; and there was a great cry in Egypt, for there was not a house where there was not one dead. He called for Moses and Aaron by night, and said, **Rise up, get out from among my people, both you and the Israelites; and go, serve the Lord, as you said. Also take your flocks and your herds**, as you have said, and be gone! And [ask your God to] bless me also".

Exodus 12: 30 – 32

We have had an exciting journey exploring the various tricks of Pharaoh to deny the children of Israel their complete freedom by trying very hard to prevent and stifle their liberation from slavery and bondage. God had declared their total freedom and the conditions that came with it and they were not to accept anything less. Now we finally come to the climax in chapter 12 of Exodus, which also happens to be the chapter in which the Passover, which represents the ransom Jesus paid to secure our redemption, is mentioned. Jesus came that we may have life and have it to the full, whilst the thief only comes to steal, kill and destroy. It is important that we know to the full, what God has called us to and to appropriate that by walking in it. Of course when we do not know, we settle for whatever is convenient, but thank God for Moses, who held on till complete freedom was attained.

We should not kid ourselves that the devil and the world around us will of their own accord leave us to our devices in fulfilling our God given dream, potential, calling and ministries. This is important because we have this false expectation that things will always be easy and that what is promised will just fall from the sky on a silver platter. We expect everyone to like us or for the church to be popular and for society including political leaders to accept our message. This is far from the truth and even history shows this not to be the case. However, it is also the reason we should be excited because the God who lives in us is greater than he who is in the world. On our own, things might appear impossible, but with God, nothing is impossible. Then all the glory can only be to God and not to our own agenda or personal scheming.

Satan has several bargains and tricks which manifest in various forms and result in a half-baked Christian walk, including **C**ounterfeit, **C**ompromise, non-**C**ommitment, dis-**C**ord (which damages **C**ommunity) and wrong attitude to **C**ash i.e. money. These five aspects address the counterfeit of carnal worship, vagueness and compromise of dilute worship, the uncommitted bargain of mixed (distant) worship, the discord (no-community) bargain of divided worship and the deceiving cash bargain of false religious worship.

This freedom must not only be restricted to bodily liberty but also in spirit and soul (mind). In fact, the biggest battle anyone will face is that of the mind. The weapons of our warfare are all given and made powerful to wage the mental battle which every believer will face on an hourly and daily basis, till we are taken up into glory.

As you will have realised by now, Pharaoh did not reveal all his tricks in one go, so it's very easy to get trapped by half truths. You may feel let off in one or two areas and be easily numbed and lulled into a false sense of security. However, God's desire as illustrated by Moses and Aaron, is that we function at the level of **C**ompleteness in true worship and ministry which appropriates the full package and not half measures. The question then arises; what does the Complete bargain which God desires, look like? Let's go back to the text so we keep this discourse within its true biblical context.

"Rise up, get out from among my people, both you and the Israelites; and go, serve the Lord, as you said. Also take your flocks and your herds, as you have said, and be gone! **And [ask your God to] bless me also.**

In this short statement by Pharaoh, we identify 5 key aspects of True and Complete Worship.

A. It always has God's word at its core ("as you said") – No Counterfeit

Now we need to be careful not to enter into the error of wishful thinking, wild imaginations and pronouncements which do not originate from the Spirit of God and His word. Pharaoh here says 'as you said', but in reality, it is based purely on what God had spoken to Moses at the burning bush and we need to be careful to hold on to what God originally spoke to us in any mission we undertake for him. The bible says in three places (Deuteronomy, Matthew and Luke), that men and women must not live on bread alone but on every word that proceeds from God's mouth. That is the foundation of everything we embark upon for and with God. Anything else is just an adventure based on a rumour and whatever you may choose to call it, but not in God's name. So many of us embark on journeys, activities and ventures, which God never sanctioned but which we have forced upon ourselves out of competition, comparison, insecurity, jealousy and envy which is a very dangerous road to take. Of course we need to learn from others but not do things because someone said so or did it.

In the book of Habakkuk, the prophet made several complaints as he beheld all the evil around him and how it appeared God was aloof to all that happened in this world. But God reminded him to write down the vision which He would show him and encouraged him to wait for it though it may appear to delay, because God's word and promises never fail. That is why we must always rely and depend on it absolutely.

B. Get out from the place of slavery – No Compromise

It will have been interesting if after all these challenges and disasters that have brought Pharaoh to his knees, Moses wanted round two of the incredible demonstrations of miracles. Imagine Moses saying to the Israelites, now we have the upper hand, let's teach them a lesson and pray more plagues from heaven and enjoy the limelight of spiritual celebrity. Alternatively, they could have decided to exact revenge and like Pharaoh, possibly initiated their own bargains to have a stake in the land of Egypt and moved from the lower class to the upper class. After all, they had served as slaves with no payment for their labour except their food. Even more tempting, could be Moses thinking, look, this throne could actually be mine and now that I have their attention, I could have what I always wanted, which was to become the ruler of these people in Egypt and possibly become the Pharaoh, given he was the adopted son of Pharaohs daughter.

These scenarios are not specifically mentioned in the bible and are only speculative, but common life experiences through observing individuals, families and nations, have shown us that these are real possibilities. Sometimes, the most dangerous period of a person, family or nation is when things seem to go smoothly after a season of challenges and difficulties, when we're likely to take our eyes off the ball. However, the message from God was clear in the original mandate, through Moses and Aaron.

Finally, Pharaoh, the pagan ruler also rehearses God's original instruction and promise to Moses. This is really important and critical because, I am fully aware that in normal life, international diplomacy and even within families, we need to be able to negotiate, which always involves both sides making compromises. That is valid and has its place as we cannot always have our way and leave the other person bitter. However, when it comes to what God has promised and commanded or a dream and vision He has specifically laid on our hearts, we must pay attention to make sure that all apparent doors and opportunities that come our way, fully align with what God originally told us. Sometimes, that involves going through a series of small open doors and opportunities but we must see them as stepping stones and not let the means become an end. As I noted in the speculative scenarios above, Pharaoh could have lifted all laws subjecting them to slavery, he could have built mansions for them and convinced them to accept that luxury instead of travelling to an uncertain desert. Whilst that will have been appealing and appeared as a blessing, it did not align with God's original intent and who knows what the outcome could be if that were an option.

With this background, let us now address the practical implications of this point. We must not become so used to slavery and the things that hold us down we begin to accept them as normal and not desire to be completely free from them. Our desire for freedom must far outweigh the bondage and traps we endure, so we can easily make the step to receiving freedom and remaining free. For example, there are people who seem to enjoy particular problems because it allows them to get continuous attention from others and any effort to move them towards overcoming these problems is confronted with statements such as "you don't know what I am going through". Of course that may well be true but it is just the fact which cannot be denied, but that fact is not always the whole truth. The truth is that God wills and has declared that we walk in freedom and victory. The question is whether we want to be free ourselves and are willing to take that step for freedom and move towards our promised destination. In the case of the Israelites, this was the land flowing with milk and honey, which was Canaan. To answer this question, let us examine, briefly, two case studies in the New Testament all involving Jesus Christ.

i. The man at the pool of Bethsaida
"After this there was a feast of the Jews, and Jesus went up to Jerusalem. Now there is in Jerusalem by the Sheep Gate a pool, which is called in Hebrew, Bethesda, having five porches. In these lay a great multitude of sick people, blind, lame, paralyzed, waiting for the moving of the water. For an angel went down at a certain time into the pool and stirred up the water; then whoever stepped in first, after the stirring of the water, was made well of whatever disease he had. Now a certain man was there who had an infirmity thirty-eight years. When Jesus saw him lying there, and knew that he already had

been in that condition a long time, He said to him, **do you want to be made well**? The sick man answered Him, Sir, I have no man to put me into the pool when the water is stirred up; but while I am coming, another steps down before me. Jesus said to him, Rise, take up your bed and walk. And immediately the man was made well, took up his bed, and walked."

John 5: 1 – 8

ii. Jesus and blind Bartimaeus

"Then they came to Jericho. As Jesus and his disciples, together with a large crowd, were leaving the city, a blind man, Bartimaeus (which means son of Timaeus), was sitting by the roadside begging. When he heard that it was Jesus of Nazareth, he began to shout, Jesus, Son of David, have mercy on me! Many rebuked him and told him to be quiet, but he shouted all the more, Son of David, have mercy on me! Jesus stopped and said, call him. So they called to the blind man, Cheer up! On your feet! He's calling you. Throwing his cloak aside, he jumped to his feet and came to Jesus. **What do you want me to do for you**? Jesus asked him. The blind man said, Rabbi, I want to see. Go, said Jesus, your faith has healed you. Immediately he received his sight and followed Jesus along the road."

Mark 10: 46 – 52

In the first encounter, the man had a choice of changing his destiny by being healed from his illness or dwelling on his past and giving all the valid and genuine reasons why his life had remained the same all those 38 years. Jesus, did not continue his narrative, but changed his story to a brighter future of freedom and liberty, where he could no longer be restricted but free to fulfil his destiny. In the second encounter, Jesus presented Bartimeaus with a choice. Of course he had been begging all his life and could have asked Jesus for alms, as most people tend to do consciously or unconsciously. Becoming so used to our circumstances and environments can begin to define our outlook on life, our choices and decisions. It was important that Jesus laid out clearly, the choice he had to make, for a brighter future. This meant being responsible for his own upkeep instead of begging for food or depending on someone to lead him around to the gate of begging and indignity. The question therefore is not whether your situation is bad, but whether you really want to see change and rise up and make the most of the opportunities that arise? In other words, will you be a victor or choose to remain a victim?

I will end this subsection with a true story I heard recently. A lady had been to a healing weekend with a Christian organisation and been miraculously healed. During the period of her ailment, she had various sources of help and support provided by the government, including a free life time pension, which we refer to as 'benefits'. Once she got healed, she felt that she was strong enough to work and to save towards her own pension, so she phoned the responsible government office to try to get herself struck off the benefits. However, they did their best to convince her not to come off this rare opportunity of a secure future. She had to insist she no longer needed such benefit if she was strong enough to work. That is the spirit and attitude of someone who really wants to be free because after all, she could rationalise and say I'll keep this free pension just in case the illness returned.

C. It is corporate (you and the Israelites) – CommUnity (No disCord)

As I write this chapter, I have read and listened on radio and television to several studies showing how individuals in modern society are becoming lonelier, in the midst of all the activities and noise surrounding us. This can be attributed to several reasons, perhaps the most important being the eroding of the nuclear and extended family to a more self-centred and inward looking society. Once close knit communities, have lost their sense of community spirit to the shocking extent that an older person could die and decompose in their home for two weeks before being found. This is particularly common in Western societies where everyone keeps to themselves and no one dares 'poke' their nose in another person's business. Whilst this sense of independence can be helpful, stretched too far, it can have severe and devastating consequences. As the introduction shows, this is true in general society and obviously within Christian communities. That is why in so many places in the bible, God constantly addresses the theme of family, unity, community, supporting one another, corporate vision and team work.

In fact, it is a direct antidote to one of the trick bargains Pharaoh was playing. He obviously had tried to drive a wedge between the men and women, the children and adults and though the bible does not say, I will not be surprised if he had tried to cause division between the leadership i.e. Moses and Aaron and the people. The best indicator of this was when Pharaoh accused them of keeping the Israelites from their work (Exodus 5: 5). As a result, he increased the workload of the people and increased their burdens, by not providing straw for making bricks. The result of course was complaining from the people and their local leaders against Moses and Aaron. It is therefore very significant for Pharaoh to be saying both you i.e. Moses and Aaron and the Israelites, go worship the Lord. Further, this is very interesting because in the original announcement, Moses said to Pharaoh; "This is what the Lord God of Israel says, Let my people go so they may make a pilgrimage for me in the desert".

Perhaps, for Aaron, this was no big deal, but not for Moses. Remember, Moses, was the adopted son of the former Pharaoh's daughter, who found him floating on the river, which therefore made him an Egyptian by rights of adoption. Moses had a choice whether to say, I've achieved my dream of freeing my people from slavery, now I can contend for the throne and enjoy everything I lost all these forty years running away and wandering in the wilderness. Now you might be wondering about all this potential speculation about Moses' possible dilemma. However, I believe this to be highly possible as we find in the book of Hebrews.

"… By faith Moses, when he had grown up, **refused to be known as the son of Pharaoh's daughter**. He chose to be mistreated along with the people of God rather than to enjoy the pleasures of sin for a short time. He regarded **disgrace for the sake of Christ as of greater value than the treasures of Egypt**, because he was looking ahead to his reward. By faith **he left Egypt, not fearing the king's anger**; he persevered because he saw him who is invisible. By faith he kept the Passover and the sprinkling of blood, so that the destroyer of the firstborn would not touch the firstborn of Israel. By faith the people passed through the Red Sea as on dry land; but when the Egyptians tried to do so, they were drowned."

Hebrews 11: 23 - 29

You see Moses had been on a faith journey right from his youth and had once left Egypt as an outlaw, when the king was angry, after he had murdered the Egyptian. However, he had to make that journey out of fear. Of course that journey had taught him everything he needed as a leader, which is beautifully captured in the book titled "Moses, the making of a leader" by Jeff Lucas. It was that journey which eventually led him to the popular 'burning bush' encounter with God and which changed his life forever. However, on this occasion, the king was not so much angry as he was scared and frightened. In a sense, Pharaoh and his people were vulnerable and Moses could have used this apparent upper hand to threaten Pharaoh with further plagues to exact his own man-made bargains. However, in the same way he had left as a murderer, not fearing the king's anger, he had to exercise his faith by leaving Egypt for good and lead the children of Israel out of slavery, towards crossing of the Red Sea just as God had commanded him. Moses will of course go on to encounter God in intimate and amazing ways, but that was not made known to him at the outset. That is why it was a journey of faith for him as well as to the rest of the children of Israel. In a way, Moses had rediscovered his true identity as an Israelite as the book of Hebrews explains.

This brings me to a few modern applications which I want to direct at leaders and people in places of authority, power and influence, including professionals who either through their words or by their life styles suggest the wrong policy of "do as I say and not as I do". There are many who will encourage people to give towards God's work and mission who themselves do not give as they demand from others. We can preach against particular sins and yet fail miserably in that same area. It's a form of self-attribution which I've seen and heard in several pulpits. Instead of first removing the log in our eyes and learning the doctrine of grace, we spend all the time bashing other preachers or our own sheep, whilst at the same time, forgetting that one day our sins could find us out. Is it not surprising that some of the feistiest campaigners against rape, fornication, homosexuality, pornography and adultery have themselves been caught out committing the same sins they preached against?

Corporate worship requires that we do not have a kind of top down

Christianity but rather a family type system where in actual fact the triangle is inverted so that the most influential bears the most responsibility and weight, which is a very humbling place to be. No part is more important than the other, and neither is any ministry less important. Those in leadership should not by default or design look down on the people they lead and by the same token, those without titles should not spend time undermining the people with responsibility for providing leadership and vision.

We started the introduction to this section with the loneliness in modern society, which has reached epidemic proportions, even in the midst of supposed prosperity and technological advancement with television, mobile phones, iPads, tablets and the internet. Unfortunately, the same can be true in Christian circles, not least among leaders. It is common to find leaders who are so lonely because they have no real close friends largely due to their 'elevated' position. Sometimes it could also be the elitist mind-set of some leaders which removes them from genuine friendships and relationships (outside of their immediate families). This could either be due to people withdrawing or fearing familiarity which is a real challenge both for the leader and the followers. Most members will not entertain a deep personal friendship with a leader for fear of losing respect through knowing too much. On the other hand, the leader might be reluctant to get too close to members either through a genuine fear of revealing too much, falling into temptation morally or even breaking confidences, which are all real dangers.

D. It is God focused (go serve the Lord) - Committed

We have been called as part of a kingdom and not a denomination, a club, clique or personalities. Whilst a local and even cultural expression of worship is important for community support and accountability, ultimately, God is to be the object and centre of our worship. Too much of Christianity has focused on non-essentials such as flattering titles, denominational barriers, mechanics and styles of worship, all of which have become a source of division in the body of Christ. So how were they to serve the Lord? Well we need to look ahead to all that transpired on their journeys through the wilderness including: learning to trust God for food, protection and survival, overcoming enemies and opposition, learning to fight, obeying His law, the building of the tabernacle, using their skills, sacrifices and worship, the glory appearing, waiting on God when Moses delayed and eventually possessing the promised land. We will pick up on sacrifices and using of their skills and material goods to serve God in the last part of this chapter. However, the story of the Israelites as they journeyed through the wilderness shows a constant tendency to take their eyes off God as their main focus and allowing other things to take first place in their lives. This cost them dearly as summarised in the book of Corinthians.

"For I do not want you to be ignorant of the fact, brothers and sisters, that our ancestors were all under the cloud and that they all passed through the sea. They were all baptized into Moses in the cloud and in the sea. They all ate the same spiritual food and drank the same spiritual drink; for they drank from the spiritual rock that accompanied them, and that rock was Christ. Nevertheless, God was not pleased with most of them; their bodies were scattered in the wilderness. Now these things occurred as examples to keep us from setting our hearts on evil things as they did. Do not be idolaters, as some of them were; as it is written: The people sat down to eat and drink and got up to indulge in revelry. We should not commit sexual immorality, as some of them did - and in one day twenty-three thousand of them died. We should not test Christ, as some of them did - and were killed by snakes. And do not grumble, as some of them did - and were killed by the destroying angel. [11] These things happened to them as examples and were written down as warnings for us, on whom the culmination of the ages has come. So, if you think you are standing firm, be careful that you don't fall!"

1 Corinthians 10: 1-12

E. It involves all we have – Cash (or money) with a mission
Finally, in Pharaohs' final and complete bargain, he spells out the last bit of the jigsaw about what true worship involves and entails. He specifically says; not only are you free to leave, but also take "…**your flocks and herds with you**". This is the cash aspect of our whole discourse to this point. Previously, Pharaoh had tried to prevent them from leaving with their personal belongings and the material things they had acquired, which will have made their sacrifice impossible. Please refer to chapter 7 for a full exposition of why this is important.

Implications – the need for balance

You will by now have noticed that the real and final deal comprised all the five aspects which Pharaoh attempted to dilute, as he bargained with Moses about their request and God's instruction for their freedom. Counterfeit (carnality), compromise, poor commitment, discord (divided community) and wrong attitude to cash (money) are all things the enemy uses to keep us from fulfilling our destiny in Him. This leads us to the final point I want to make which is the need to lead a balanced life in our personal, social and spiritual walk. A false balance leads to some form of 'disease' which makes us not function to maximum capacity. This is manifest in several seemingly innocuous ways by churches, families and individuals and even nations because we place emphasis on one or more of these five aspects to the detriment of the others. In extreme cases, we look down on others who equally over emphasise other aspects to the neglect of the rest. The result is that we're kept in a state of flux, stagnancy and never attaining to or even growing towards maturity, perfection and wholeness. That is not what Christ has in mind for us and in the last two chapters, we will explore this within a New Testament context, centred around the mission of Jesus Christ to humanity and in particular His church and how we need to appropriate these promises to live an abundant Christian life in freedom and liberty in all aspects of our lives.

CHAPTER 9 FREEDOM FIGHTER
'The Man, His Mission, Manifesto, Ministry and Message'

Throughout history, whole groups, tribes, families and nations have faced oppression from others, who like Pharaoh sought to deprive them of their freedom. However, human beings have within them a desire to be free and have been prepared to pay the price to achieve their freedoms. These include the American war for independence, independence from colonial powers, fight against slave trade, fight against Nazism and fascism, fight against communism, the Arab spring and apartheid in South Africa. None of these have happened in a vacuum, but have often been carried on the shoulders of brave men and women who stood up against oppression. These were mere mortals with a mission and burning desire for freedom, who eventually prevailed against all the odds. Even as I write, there are still places around the world struggling for their freedoms including Palestinians, North Korea, brutal dictators in the Middle East and Africa, all with key individuals leading their fight for freedom. Sadly, on some occasions, these fights for freedom have turned sour after apparent freedom had been attained, as was the case in South Sudan, Eritrea, Libya and Egypt.

No matter how famous these individuals are, there is a more important personality who roamed the streets of this earth to secure a more significant freedom of eternal proportions for all of humanity. Unlike Pharaoh, this individual does not bargain our freedoms away, but rather reinforces them if we will yield to Him. Most people's view of Christianity is one of rules and restriction of our freedoms, but that is far from the truth. This concept of freedom was so important in the Old Testament that God instituted the Jubilee which we will discuss in a bit more detail later in this chapter. Physical servitude and debt were both classified as slavery and God was desperate to show them how vital it was for them to guard the freedom which had been secured for them in Egypt and subsequently fulfilled in Christ (Isaiah chapter 61 and Luke chapter 4). That is why I have chosen to 'nick name' him the Freedom Fighter because he fought and paid the ultimate price of a humiliating death on the cross to secure our freedom. Further, he rose again from the dead and lives on to sustain it for all eternity. In this chapter, we will evaluate this man, his mission, manifesto, ministry and message.

v 14 – 17: "Jesus returned to Galilee in the power of the Spirit, and news about him spread through the whole countryside. He was teaching in their synagogues, and everyone praised him. He went to Nazareth, where he had been brought up, and on the Sabbath day he went into the synagogue, as was his custom. He stood up to read, and the scroll of the prophet Isaiah was handed to him. Unrolling it, he found the place where it is written:

v 18 – 19: "The Spirit of the Lord is on me, because he has anointed me **to proclaim good news to the poor. He has sent me to proclaim freedom for the prisoners and recovery of sight for the blind, to set the oppressed free, to proclaim the year of the Lord's favour.**"

v 20 – 21: "Then he rolled up the scroll, gave it back to the attendant and sat down. The eyes of everyone in the synagogue were fastened on him. He began by saying to them, **today this scripture is fulfilled** in your hearing."

Luke 4:14-21

The context of this portion of the bible is that Jesus had just won one of His many great victories over Satan in overcoming temptations along the lines of the lust of the eyes, the lust of the flesh and the pride of life. Prior to this, He had been baptised in water by John the Baptist, baptised and anointed by the Holy Spirit. In that process of water and Holy Spirit baptism, He was affirmed and confirmed by the heavenly Father as the only begotten Son in whom God was well pleased and more significantly, the one we need to listen to. Therefore it's important that we pay particular attention to what Jesus Christ had to say after these events. Not only did He overcome the devil here, but he also experienced our infirmities and our human temptations and came out victorious. The bible says he returned to Galilee full of the Spirit and so whatever, Jesus says here does carry a lot of weight and substance. It is in this context that Jesus Christ laid out His great manifesto and mission towards all of humanity and defined His life's purpose.

Therefore verse 18 begins with the incredible statement, "The Spirit of the sovereign Lord is upon me" which is implied by what He is mandated and empowered to accomplish on behalf of the poor, broken hearted, captive and bound. Interestingly, the first four chapters of Luke are filled with a consistent theme of the Holy Spirit's work in this regard and builds up to this climax in Luke 4:18. These are outlined briefly for the reader for personal study later on.

He was **C**onceived by the Spirit   - Luke 1:35-40   - Incarnation
He was **C**ommissioned by the Spirit - Luke 3:22-23   - Calling
He **C**onquered by the Spirit   - Luke 4:1-2   - Victory
He **C**ontinued in the Power of the Spirit - Luke 4:14   - Mission

Now let us explore briefly, his manifesto, ministry and His message under three main contexts. The first context addresses the list of people he seeks to reach and with what message.

A. Good news to the poor

I'm not sure if you have ever experienced extreme lack in your life and struggled to make ends meet. The news this week in the UK, as I write this section, shows an increase in the number of poor working families. In dealing with this scripture, there are dangers with two extreme positions which we need to get out of the way:

(i) The first is limiting the poor and captives and blind and oppressed to physical and social states. But Jesus said in Revelation 3 vs 17 that "you think you are rich and have need of nothing and yet do not know that you are poor, naked and blind". He was referring to spiritual blindness and spiritual poverty.

(ii) The second extreme is not taking a stand for the poor and vulnerable and in fact using the gospel to justify poverty in the name of obtaining riches in heaven. However, Jesus said, whatever we do for the poor is done unto Him, so we cannot wait till we get to heaven.

The question therefore arises, what was Jesus really saying? Perhaps a personal illustration will do. During my life time, there have been times when I did not have enough food to eat or money to spend. The people who were a blessing to me were not those who only showed sympathy verbally, though it was well meant. It was actually those who did something about it by sharing their food and resources with me and honestly, these people hold a special place in my heart because they responded to my specific needs. Let's consider these three scenarios:

i. What is good news to a starving family in a country or community experiencing famine? **Answer -** food aid or teaching them to irrigate and maximise the output from the land.

ii. What is good news to a debt ridden parent whose house is about to be repossessed? **Answer -** debt forgiveness. Of course, I believe it's important for everyone to live within their means.

iii. What is good news to a worker made redundant from his or her job? **Answer -** Employment.

Therefore, what does Jesus mean with the phrase 'preaching good news to the poor'? Specifically He comes to announce good news of release to the captives, recovery of sight to the blind and liberation for the oppressed. The Jews at this time were living under Roman captivity and subjected to severe political oppression as well as religious oppression from the Pharisees and Sadducees. In those days, the people will have been used to hearing of judgment upon all who failed in God's laws from their priests and prophets. However, none of these priests and prophets could help them obey these laws. In fact they were subject to breaking the law themselves. Jesus not only comes with a message of hope, but announces the solution to mankind's problem. So when you think of Good News to the poor, think of what Jesus did for you that you could not or cannot do for yourself.

The message was good news because they were not only saved from sin but elevated past the powerful Roman Empire to become citizens of the kingdom of God. This is definitely good news to a people under spiritual and political oppression. That is why the gospel has always been attractive to the poor, weak and vulnerable, because its message is liberating, freeing us to live beyond all forms of control - spiritually, philosophically, mentally and emotionally even when we face physical oppression.

In general science, there is a fundamental principle called **diffusion** which affects all systems including your body. Substances or compounds will be transported from an area of higher concentration or higher pressure to a place of lower concentration or pressure. The difference between the two areas is called concentration or pressure gradient. Without this gradient, your air freshener is useless. The food you eat and drink will be digested but just remain in your stomach and intestines and you could die from starvation or dehydration. If you took paracetamol, it will never be absorbed to the site of action to cure your pain. The 'poor in spirit' allow a gradient by acknowledging their need in order to receive from Christ and trust Him for their salvation and eternal security. They are dependent on only Him to satisfy their spiritual hunger and to fill the vacuum in their hearts. When we don't, our lives become empty and unfulfilling. Even legitimate religious activities such as prayer and fasting without Christ as the motivation are meaningless and will lead us nowhere.

In addition, the good news is that Jesus came looking for the sick, the maimed, the lame, the bruised, the broken hearted, the wretched wanderer, the poor, the forgotten and the prisoner. Further, He also came for the rich but lonely person whose riches cannot secure their eternal destiny. He came for the powerful leader whose insecurity makes him or her feel threatened even by the lowest ranked employee. These people, when they are willing to accept their need of Christ will be set free. This is good news to the poor and I believe it with absolute certainty.

B. Deliverance (freedom) for the captives and recovery of sight to the blind

When I see prisons in certain parts of the world on the news, with flat screens, nice showers and snooker tables, it can feel like prison is a nice place. However, if you visit an ancient prison, for example, in certain old medieval castles, you get a different picture. Prisoners were kept in dungeons deep below ground and chained to each other or to the wall with little or no light and zero chance of escaping. A deep and dark dungeon keeps you stuck and slowly destroys your sight and health. With no chance of escape, your only options are a pardon or a more powerful army coming to your rescue. Jesus says in His mission statement from Luke 4 vs 18 "You can be set free from captivity and overcome its effect on your vision and life in general because he comes to proclaim your freedom by overruling the captor. It does not matter how entrenched the captivity is and how extensive the damage, He is powerful enough to secure our freedom and recover what is lost.

Deliverance (freedom) for the captive implies pardon and is a picture of a prisoner of war being set free by a king or a president granting pardon to someone who is lawfully guilty. It's important to note that like Pharaoh in the book of Exodus, the devil and all the things that seek to hold us in bondage do not grant pardons. Have you ever seen a drug dealer saying to his client, you've bought too much crack cocaine or heroin today so come back next year? Only the police and the law can intervene to set him free if at all possible. As I write this section, Europe is reeling under the burden of human traffickers who transport desperate asylum seekers across the ocean and abandon them to their fate with no crew. Within the spate of a few days, two such vessels filled with men, women and children have been rescued by the Italian Coast Guard. In Thailand and Malaysia, several mass graves have been discovered of desperate migrants killed by human traffickers who hold these people hostage and demand ransoms from their families. These are wicked people with little or no conscience for human dignity.

Jesus addresses the key effect of living in a dark dungeon, which is blindness. So he says I don't only free you from prison, I also help your poor sight to be restored. "Medically, underground living results in the lack of exposure to natural light which increases the risk of vitamin D deficiency, leading to bone diseases such as rickets and osteoporosis as well potential chronic conditions such as hypertension. Blindness can also mean ignorance which is a dangerous prison to be in. Imagine getting lost or stranded in a thick jungle for several years with no news and suddenly being found by a stranger and having to catch up on the news and all the advancements in life. Finally, blindness can be a lack of vision and perspective even after we're saved.

Now let's turn briefly to Isaiah 49:24-25. If you find yourself in a situation which you feel cannot change, think again, because there is a God who is stronger than the situation that imprisons you. Isaiah here says even the **lawful captive shall be delivered**, so even if you feel you deserve your bad predicament, He still wants to set you free if only you will let Him (Psalm 146:7-8). God can set the captives free and restore their sight. If you are here and you pray for people to be free from darkness, use these two scriptures (Isaiah 49 and Psalm 146) to help you prevail before God and against all the enemy's traps. You do not have to be on drugs but whatever it is, Jesus comes to set you free from that bondage and to restore whatever you've lost as a result. Maybe you've lost a big chunk of your life to various habits that have affected your mental and emotional wellbeing and even your decision making. Jesus can change all that and restore you to newness of life. You may be crippled by fear including the fear of failure and of the future which can dim your perspective on life. He's proclaimed your liberty and secured recovery of your sight so you can see life from His point of view.

C. Freedom from oppression

There are certain historical words that send shivers down our spines and no one likes to be associated with them; for example the slave trade, holocaust, apartheid, racism and segregation and anti-Semitism. These oppressive periods were so traumatic that the scars are still visible today. The encouraging contrast as we mentioned in the introduction is that we also know of leaders who fought to end such oppression including; William Wilberforce, Abraham Lincoln, Nelson Mandela and Pope John Paul. These names remind us that good always triumphs over evil and therefore we keep a hopeful perspective.

This mission of Jesus, speaks of those whose lives are made hard and bitter under severe burdens, and whose spirits are broken and crushed beneath a weight of accumulated ills. Freedom from oppression is emancipation from all forms of slavery. As we have read from Exodus, there were four main characteristics of this oppression. It was imposed (forced labour), ruthless, harsh and resulted in bitterness. However, God intervened miraculously by sending Moses and we have a greater than Moses, in the person of Jesus Christ. In Jesus' day, there were also four different levels of oppression: (i) political oppression from the Romans; (ii) religious oppression from the Pharisees; (iii) physical and emotional oppression from sickness and disease and (iv) spiritual oppression from sin and the devil.

Jesus did not directly confront the Roman Empire but by addressing the remaining three, he set in motion a movement that eventually influenced the Roman Empire and led to a great missionary movement from Europe. Jesus confronted the Pharisees who got offended even when someone was healed on the Sabbath. He healed the sick and delivered people from demonic oppression both of which are part of the gospel message (Luke 4: 33 - 35, 38 - 41).

What are the things you do not desire that oppress you and cause bruising to your soul and make your heart bitter? It could be entrenched sinful habits, accusations of the devil, guilt and depression. It could be difficulties whilst growing up or suffering the consequences of our parents' mistakes. These things can become strong holds and a constant thorn in our flesh unless we turn them over to Christ who wants to set us free. It might require forgiving and letting go of some painful past experiences. It does not justify those wrongs as being ok, because they are not and God takes a very dim view of such issues. However, you might be crying out in desperation to be free from these yokes of oppression. The truth is that like the children of Israel in Egypt, God hears and responds to your heart cry. If you are wondering, whether God is interested in the things that afflict us emotionally, physically and mentally listen to this supporting mission statement of Jesus as mentioned by Peter.

"How God anointed Jesus Christ of Nazareth with the Holy Ghost and with power, who went about doing good and healing all who were oppressed by the devil, for God was with Him."

Acts 10:38

This is part of the gospel package and it is a scandal when the church restricts the message of the gospel to only repenting of sin and then coming to church, ready for heaven. Jesus wants to save you from the prison of sin and free you from all other forms of oppression and bondage so you can be an effective witness to release others.

D. Healing for the broken hearted
When I first arrived in the UK, I saw this mission statement in the first church I visited which eventually became my place of worship: **"Bringing the Healing Love of God to a Hurting World"**. This for me captures the heart of what God wants for the cities, communities, families and individuals in our world. Do we as believers contribute to the pain of an already hurting world or if you are not yet a born again believer, are you rejecting the healing that God freely provides to you?

Jesus was not anointed only to sit in one place just enjoying lovely worship, sound theology, vigorous apologetic debate, powerful prayer and sacrificial fasting. On the contrary, He was sent out to do specific things. Likewise, we have also been sent and it does not take place in church only on a Sunday. We come to be fed, encouraged and equipped to go face a hurting and lost world. The Greek word translated healing means to cure or make whole. Broken hearted means: to crush completely, break in pieces or bruised. In its true context, the phrase refers to those whose hearts are crushed over their sin, shattered by their failures and sorry often for the same thing that easily besets them. Isaiah 61 uses the word 'bind up' which is very revealing because it depicts wrapping firmly together to avoid falling apart so it heals completely.

Who is Jesus referring to, in other words, who needs healing?
i. Those broken and sorry over their sin;
ii. Those haunted by painful past mistakes and scars which cause regret, guilt and anger;
iii. Those who are wounded and hurting. This last example is important because it is quite a well-known observation that hurting people are prone to hurting others as their fragile hearts cannot handle the pain of being hurt again. That is why there is a tendency for wounded people to carry their hurt into relationships including

marriage and end up destroying the very people whom they love, sometimes with devastating consequences, especially for children.

I once heard the lovely story of a woman on Christian television. This woman who had been abused as a child by the men she trusted, was suspicious of any male who came close around her literal physical space, even at work, no matter how genuine they were. Now these were not people interested in a romantic relationship but literally people who came near to her within close centimetre radius. But who could blame her, she was a wounded person protecting her physical space to avoid sexual exploitation and emotional abuse. One day, she worked with a male colleague for hours and the thoughts and fear of being sexually attacked never occurred to her even once. Then she said, "**suddenly I realised God had healed my heart and delivered me from the pain of my past**". This is what Charles Wesley, the great hymn writer called "breaking the power of cancelled sin" in his famous hymn "And can it be, that I should gain an interest in the Saviour's love". Jesus not only forgives your acknowledged sin, He also has the power to bind up the wounds caused by the effects of sin both by you and sins against you.

Ruth Graham, one of Billy Graham's daughters has written a book titled "**In Every Pew Sits a Broken Heart**" and I encourage you to refer to it if you are able to purchase a copy. In talking about this book during a television interview on Christian Broadcasting Network (CBN), she noted that it was important to reach out to people beyond what they project outwardly as she shared the stories of her own personal difficulties even though she had, perhaps the most famous Christian of our generation as her dad[11]. We've all come to Christ travelling on different roads, some more difficult than others. Some come to Christ after very painful and traumatic experiences that will take anyone to breaking point. We all come messed up and the tendency is to remain messed up. At the same time, we in church can make it worse for people on the road to recovery. A little boy was sitting in his push chair in church during worship, clapping and making happy noises. Then the parent turned and screamed with an angry voice, stop that, you are in church, at which point the little toddler started to cry. Can you guess what his parent's response was? That's better! When I first read this story on the internet, my response was 'goodness me, church is not meant to be a place of misery and God help us if we make it that way.

Another person was invited to church and responded in horror, "Church? I already felt horrible about myself before I went there and they made me feel worse about myself. This is completely alien to the good news Jesus came to preach. It does not mean He tolerated sin. Obviously this might well be a subjective view based on a few experiences but it's still not the impression we should be projecting. Jesus' message was "the kingdom of heaven is near, repent and believe in the gospel". When he met the woman caught in adultery, he said "neither do I condemn you, go and sin no more". Do you think the woman was proud of her sin? Did she have the power to overcome sin without Christ? The answer is a big fat no. However, there is no record of the man who committed adultery with her or the people who tried to stone her being forgiven and healed because they did not acknowledge their sin and their need for freedom.

In more than 25 years of active preaching, I have come to realise that most people are already broken, worn out and weary before they venture into church. My dogmatic and religious upbringing always tempts me to label them but listen to what Jesus said in Matthew 12:15-21.

"Aware of this, Jesus withdrew from that place. A large crowd followed him, and he healed all who were ill. He warned them not to tell others about him. This was to fulfil what was spoken through the prophet Isaiah: Here is my servant whom I have chosen, the one I love, in whom I delight; I will put my Spirit on him, and he will proclaim justice to the nations. He will not quarrel or cry out; no one will hear his voice in the streets. **A bruised reed he will not break, and a smouldering wick he will not snuff out**, till he has brought justice through to victory. In his name the nations will put their hope."

Matthew 12: 15-21

Remember that the Greek word broken hearted also means bruised. Jesus does not give knockout punches to those at breaking point, but rather, He heals and restores them. Interestingly, the context in

Matthew 12 was about the religious leaders opposing this very mission of Jesus because He had healed on the Sabbath day. We are like the prodigal son, who blow our Father's unlimited resource of mercy, grace, forgiveness and kindness and it's within God's right to judge us. However, the father did not let him complete his sentence, when he was requesting to become a servant. Rather, the father was willing to give him another chance. Those of us with children will never dream of disowning them even if they don't do what we say. Why do we think God will do differently in this period of grace?

We should definitely not promote and encourage sin, because the bible says "woe to him who calls good evil and evil good". However, we should proclaim the good news that if people acknowledge their sin and repent, they will be healed. What about the wounds caused by our rebellion towards God? Well as we've read from Matthew, he does not push you over the edge. In Matthew 12 Jesus says the exact opposite. When you are bruised and hurt, he does not crush you into oblivion. When you are burning low, He does not quench your lamp. On the contrary, He forgives, cleanses, heals and restores. That is why His message is good news.

Why then do people act like there's no healing and no remedy for the tragedies of humanity? Even in church, we try to be like professionals who are in control all the time. Let me paint a picture with an illustration. A highly paid personal assistant in a global company headquarters, who is having personal problems was weeping by their office desk when the phone rang. The person picked the phone and in dramatic fashion, smiles broadly and says oh hello, you are through to Jo Bloggs International Limited, how can I help you today? After helping the customer, which is what you will expect of a professional, the personal assistant ends the conversation as follows "super, you have a brilliant day and speak to you again soon darling. As soon as this individual put the handset down they go straight back into their self-pity and crying. That is ok in a secular professional setting, but before God, it is just whitewashing and studio make-up. What He yearns for is, please just allow me to cry with you and in the process heal your pain. Listen to God's complaint in the book of Jeremiah

"The harvest is past, the summer has ended, and we are not saved. Since my people are crushed, I am crushed; I mourn, and horror grips me. **Is there no balm in Gilead? Is there no physician there? Why then is there no healing for the wound of my people?**"

Jeremiah 8:21-22

"Go up to Gilead and get balm, Virgin Daughter Egypt. **But you try many medicines in vain; there is no healing for you**".

Jeremiah 46:11.

Why do we think we can know true healing and wholeness without letting Christ be at the centre of our lives? We have to come to the point like the prodigal son and say I have sinned against God, not the church or the pastor. Run to Him and you'll be surprised how much change He will bring to your life.

E. Royal Favour – Jubilee (Luke 4: 18-21, Isaiah 61:1-8)

Most people on meagre monthly salaries run short of money by the 15th day of a five week month such as January or July and usually yearn for their next pay cheque to arrive. We have a saying in my native Ghanaian language that translates quite literally "even when it gets worse, it's not as bad as pay day". Debt and lack are like a prison that cripples to the point of controlling your whole being (mentally, emotionally). Debt is a form of slavery which the bible says we should avoid. God, the creator of the world and all mankind has always had an interest in what happens to His people. There is a false perception in the world and sometimes in church, that God somehow hated the world so much after Adam's sin, that he washed His hands off as an absentee father. However, this is far from the truth and alien to the bible because He seeks our interests and what is to our benefit. Don't forget that God provided skin to replace the leaves Adam and Eve used to cover their nakedness.

The fundamental truth that underpins most established democracies, particularly in the Western world is the Judaeo-Christian principle that all men and women are created equal in the image of God and therefore deserve to live in freedom. Of course, this has unfortunately been interpreted to mean licence which is a dangerous phenomenon that has led to shocking moral decay in Western countries, including the redefinition of marriage, abortion and in some cases promotion of euthanasia. In the 1970's and 80's there was a paedophile group called Paedophile Information Exchange which attempted to lobby government to legalise sex with underage children. Interestingly, there has been a recent exposure of significant abuse of young boys and girls by very powerful political and social figures which is very sad and scandalous. That is what happens when we interpret freedom to mean licence.

The final part of Jesus' mission and manifesto is Jubilee, which He described as the acceptable year of the Lord or the day of the Lord's favour. We will tackle the characteristics of Jubilee on three levels.

- Practice of Jubilee   – The reality in the Old Testament
- Promise of Jubilee   – The expectation from the Old Testament
- Pursuit of Jubilee   – The fulfilment and application in the New Testament (you and I).

1. Practice of Jubilee (Leviticus 25: 8-54)
A section of Leviticus chapter 25 is reproduced below:

"Count off seven Sabbath years - seven times seven years - so that the seven Sabbath years amount to a period of forty-nine years. Then have the trumpet sounded everywhere on the tenth day of the seventh month; on the Day of Atonement sound the trumpet throughout your land. Consecrate the fiftieth year and proclaim liberty throughout the land to all its inhabitants. It shall be a jubilee for you; each of you is to return to your family property and to your own clan. The fiftieth year shall be a jubilee for you; do not sow and do not reap what grows of itself or harvest the untended vines. For it is a jubilee and is to be holy for you; eat only what is taken directly from the fields. In this Year of Jubilee everyone is to return to their own property. If you sell land to any of your own people or buy land from them, do not take advantage of each other. You are to buy from your own people on the basis of the number of years since the Jubilee. And they are to sell to you on the basis of the number of years left for harvesting crops. When the years are many, you are to increase the price, and when the years are few, you are to decrease the price, because what is really being sold to you is the number of crops. Do not take advantage of each other, but fear your God. I am the LORD your God. Follow my decrees and be careful to obey my laws, and you will live safely in the land. Then the land will yield its fruit, and you will eat your fill and live there in safety. You may ask, "What will we eat in the seventh year if we do not plant or harvest our crops? I will send you such a blessing in the sixth year that the land will yield enough for three years. While you plant during the eighth year, you will eat from the old crop and will continue to eat from it until the harvest of the ninth year comes in. The land must not be sold permanently, because the land is mine and you reside in my land as foreigners and strangers. Throughout the land that you hold as a possession, you must provide for the redemption of the land. If one of your fellow Israelites becomes poor and sells some of their property, their nearest relative is to come and redeem what they have sold. If, however, there is no one to redeem it for them but later on they prosper and acquire sufficient means to redeem it themselves, they are to determine the value for the years since they sold it and refund the balance to the one to whom they sold it; they can then go back to their own property. But if they do not acquire the means to repay, what was sold will remain in the possession of the buyer until the Year of Jubilee. It will be returned in the Jubilee, and they can then go back to their property."

Leviticus 8: 8 - 28

The Jubilee was proclaimed every 50 years on the Day of Atonement and several things happened which are summarised below, all words beginning with 'R';
Rest: from work and slavery
Rest: for the land to recover (a form of Sabbath)
Release: from debt and slavery
Return: to family and inheritance
Restoration: of identity (family and land)
Redemption: of self, others and property

The institution and celebration of jubilee reveals the character of:
a. A God of justice interested in the poor and vulnerable in society.
b. The Creator and Provider whom we can trust and depend on to supply all our needs.

c. A God of mercy and grace who gives a second chance even when we don't deserve it.

2. Promise of Jubilee

For us the promise of Jubilee (Acceptable Year of the Lord or the Year of the Lord's favour) as found in Christ is a Divine Exchange initiated by God. Jesus quotes from Isaiah 61: 1 - 8 which is a promise to the people of Israel and mentions some important words which we will pick up on in the second context of Jesus' mission statement.

3. Pursuit of Jubilee

Under the current dispensation, favour in Jubilee extends beyond physical and material benefits and involves all of our inheritance in Christ. Jesus was wounded for our transgressions, bruised for our iniquities, the chastisement that brought us peace was on Him and by His stripes we are healed (Isaiah 53:1-8) which is the 'divine exchange' referred to in the previous section. Just like in Jubilee, He paid the ransom for our slavery to sin and redeemed us back to freedom. We still enjoy the 'divine exchange' because He died that we might live. He became sin, that we might be made the righteousness of God. He became poor that we might be rich. He was rejected that we might be accepted in Him. This is excessive favour and that is why it is good news to the poor. All we contributed was repenting, believing and accepting that what He has provided is enough. Please read Ephesians chapter 1 verses 3 - 8; and Ephesians chapter 2 verses 8 – 10 for an exposition of the inheritance and blessings we have in Christ. The song writer said:

"He paid the debt He did not owe, I owed a debt I could not pay, I needed someone to wash my sins away. Now I can sing a brand new song, amazing grace. Lord Jesus paid the debt that I could never pay".

The problem is that most of us think we can do more to deserve this favour and God is saying drop it because I give it freely and lavishly. Most of us struggle with this because we believe that the more negative we can be about ourselves, the more spiritual we become. In most of Romans chapter 1 and chapter 2, the judgment of God on sin is the main theme, however, right in the midst of these two chapters, in Romans chapter 2 verse 4, Paul says "the grace or goodness of God leads to repentance". This grace when experienced, in reality does not encourage or grant a licence to sin, but makes you enter into God's rest from sin and empowers you to live in freedom and in victory.

The second context of Luke 4: 14 – 21 is that Jesus was reading from Isaiah chapter 61 verbatim and therefore it's important to quote it here.

"The Spirit of the Sovereign LORD is on me, because the LORD has anointed me to proclaim good news to the poor. He has sent me to bind up the broken hearted, to proclaim freedom for the captives and release from darkness for the prisoners, to proclaim the year of the LORD's favour and the day of vengeance of our God, to comfort all who mourn, and provide for those who grieve in Zion - to bestow on them a crown of beauty instead of ashes, the oil of joy instead of mourning, and a garment of praise instead of a spirit of despair. They will be called oaks of righteousness, a planting of the LORD for the display of his splendour. They will rebuild the ancient ruins and restore the places long devastated; they will renew the ruined cities that have been devastated for generations. Strangers will shepherd your flocks; foreigners will work your fields and vineyards. And you will be called priests of the LORD, you will be named ministers of our God. You will feed on the wealth of nations, and in their riches you will boast. Instead of your shame you will receive a double portion, and instead of disgrace you will rejoice in your inheritance. And so you will inherit a double portion in your land, and everlasting joy will be yours."

The first two chapters have been addressed above and are the ones Jesus quoted but that is where we tend to stop. However, there is more after we have experienced the good news and been restored to freedom. This comprises His ministry and message which is what the Holy Spirit does in bringing us to maturity and into His likeness as we share in His divine nature. There is a striking similarity with

Leviticus 25 as listed below.
- **Beauty** for ashes,
- **Joy** instead of mourning,
- **Praise** instead of despair,
- **Rebuild** ancient ruins,
- **Restore** the places long devastated,
- **Renew** ruined cities.
- **Joy** instead of shame
- **Double** portion of inheritance

These lead nicely into the third context of Jesus' mission statement. The third context of Jesus' mission statement which can be easily missed is as follows; Jesus said, **"Today, this scripture is fulfilled in your ears"**. Of course He was referring to Himself so we do ourselves and God a great disservice when we defer everything about our salvation and redemption into the future and rob ourselves of the enormous blessing and potential of abundant life that Christ has deposited within us and for which He died. We will tackle this abundant life to finish off this book in the next and final chapter.

For now however, the challenge for us believers is not whether you believe you are saved but whether you can live and walk in freedom and in God's favour every day. Whether we believe it or not, Jesus said, 'today' this scripture of good news, proclaiming freedom and the year of the Lord's favour (Jubilee) is fulfilled in your ears. You have to decide whether it is only a rumour or it will be reality in your life today and until the day we meet with Him in the air. Now let's turn our attention in the last chapter, to why God desires to set us free and give us liberty.

CHAPTER 10 FREEDOM'S PURPOSE

"It was for freedom that Christ has set us free, no longer to be subject to a yoke of slavery"

John Gibson

"... Stand firm in the liberty wherewith Christ has set you free, and do not let yourselves be burdened again by a yoke of slavery"

Paul the Apostle

"There is no passion to be found playing small - in settling for a life that is less than the one you are capable of living." - **Our inheritance**

Nelson Mandela

"For to be free is not merely to cast off one's chains, but to live in a way that respects and enhances the freedom of others." – **Our responsibility**

Nelson Mandela

I hope and pray that you have been inspired and also challenged to live a life of complete and total freedom in every aspect of your life. God has a plan and purpose for each of our lives and He did not just save us from sin, just so we exist in a vacuum but empowered us to fulfil our potential in Christ. God has deposited so much in us, and He yearns and desires to see all of it expressed to bring praise and glory to His name. It should be our desire, and expectation that we will enjoy these blessings that accompany salvation. The purpose of freedom according to Paul is found in the book of Galatians: "stand firm in this liberty and no longer to be subject to a yoke of slavery". (Galatians 5: 1). A yoke of slavery can manifest itself in several forms. In the case of the church in Galatians, they were being held back by a restriction to religious rites and traditions that made the gospel and power of God lose its cutting edge and intended impact upon their lives.

Freedom is a necessity and a fact of life both in the physical and in the spiritual. Therefore, as I prayed and meditated about the best way to finish this book, there was nothing better than, the primary mission of Jesus Christ and the abundant life which comes through Him. It was He who said, "... we will know the truth, (which is embodied in Himself), that will set us free". This freedom was so important to God, He was prepared to pay the price, through Jesus Christ to purchase our liberty. It was Him (Jesus) who said the following and I quote:

"The thief comes only to steal and kill and destroy; **I have come that they may have life, and have it to the full**. I am the good shepherd. The good shepherd lays down his life for the sheep. The hired hand is not the shepherd and does not own the sheep. So when he sees the wolf coming, he abandons the sheep and runs away. Then the wolf attacks the flock and scatters it. The man runs away because he is a hired hand and cares nothing for the sheep".

John 10:10-13

The key portion we will focus on to finish is verse 10b, which in the authorised King James Version reads ".... I am come that they might have life and that they might have it more abundantly". The New International Version puts it this way: "I have come that they may have life and have it to the full" What is this life and how can we have it to the full? We have covered in the previous chapter, the mission of Jesus Christ, which ended on the note of Isaiah 61, spelling out how the ministry of Jesus doesn't stop after we become saved. We can get so used to getting saved and only waiting to get to heaven to enjoy eternal life to the full. Yet, the bible says "we have eternal life now within us", and will be further consummated when we are finally united with Jesus in glorified bodies. In the meantime, He desires for us to continuously grow into his likeness and walking in the newness of life, experiencing and enjoying the things that accompany salvation.

A few things emerge, which we need to address, before we wrap up. There is abundant life better and greater than we've become accustomed to and we need to yearn to grow deeper and higher into this life. There are depths and heights in God, which He desires to take us. I dare say God wants to take us on an adventure of growth and maturity, that may sometimes feel challenging but worth the trip.

Of course, there is always the danger of us taking things to two very dangerous extremes. Firstly, some take this to mean something beyond faith in Jesus Christ alone to secure our salvation, in other words, believing that the death, burial and resurrection of Jesus was not enough to make us sons of God. That is a done deal and was accomplished by Jesus Christ once for all for sin. Secondly, others will take it to the opposite extreme and take this to mean licence because we're saved by grace, and where sin abounds, there grace abounds even more. Both extremes are wrong and dangerous, and lead to actual bondage and as the writer of Hebrews puts it "crucifying the son all over again".

The freedom we're talking about has to do with Jesus Christ living his life through us. It's about Him showing forth his victory, power and authority through us to a world that wants nothing of Him but which needs this freedom that only He can give. Is it not interesting that God used Moses to deliver the children of Israel and yet they went round the wilderness for 40 years before inheriting the Promised Land, when in actual fact, it could have taken them just 11 days journey via a straight route. Though their long journey through the wilderness served other purposes, this was not the original intent and though they had been delivered from Egypt, they did not fully enjoy the freedom for which they were delivered. They spent 40 years wandering until the unbelieving generation had all died, and God could use the next generation, led by Joshua and Caleb to enter the Promised Land. Of course we know that all things work out for good, but the warning for us, according to Paul, is that their experiences were "written down as an example for us", who have experienced the real deal.

"For I do not want you to be ignorant of the fact, brothers, that our forefathers were all under the cloud and that they all passed through the sea. They were all baptized into Moses in the cloud and in the sea. They all ate the same spiritual food and drank the same spiritual drink; for they drank from the spiritual rock that accompanied them, and that rock was Christ. Nevertheless, God was not pleased with most of them; their bodies were scattered over the desert. Now these things occurred as examples to keep us from setting our hearts on evil things as they did. Do not be idolaters, as some of them were; as it is written: The people sat down to eat and drink and got up to indulge in pagan revelry. We should not commit sexual immorality, as some of them did--and in one day twenty-three thousand of them died. We should not test the Lord, as some of them did--and were killed by snakes. And do not grumble, as some of them did--and were killed by the destroying angel. These things happened to them as examples and were written down as warnings for us, on whom the fulfilment of the ages has come. So, if you think you are standing firm, be careful that you don't fall!"

1 Corinthians 10: 1 - 12

The point of Paul's comments here is that we don't squander our freedom but remain and flourish in it and not to take it for granted. That is the purpose of freedom. The late Dr Myles Munroe has addressed this purpose and responsibilities of freedom in his book, the Burden of Freedom. In dealing with the need to move beyond wilderness and slave mentality he made this point and I quote: "Let us learn our lessons in the wilderness so we can handle the responsibility of Canaan. The principle is that transformation is more important to God than relocation. Mental freedom is more important than physical freedom"[2]

As noted earlier, freedom is a necessity in life and a deep seated desire that is ingrained in all human cultures, even those living under brutal dictatorships. Throughout human existence, men and women have fought for and struggled to obtain freedom for themselves and on behalf of others.

However, some of these leaders, eventually turned out to become brutal dictators, who caused more havoc after they had achieved their desired first taste of freedom. Some were slave owners even though they fought for freedom from other forms of oppression from colonial powers. They forgot there was more beyond the initial proclaiming of freedom and only viewed it from their own narrow minded point of view. Some newly independent countries who fought long battles only managed to turn on themselves, resulting in protracted civil wars. Of course, some of these events, were a legacy of long years of colonial, political, mental and emotional enslavement, which meant that the responsibilities that came with freedom and liberty, after years of domination were not well managed. Others faced chaos because the oppressor sowed seeds of disunity by dividing so they could rule for so long, that by the time freedom was eventually achieved, the reality of their real divisions, hidden by the oppression begun to show up.

However, the fact still remains, that freedom is a necessary human experience which is a great privilege but which brings with it huge responsibilities both for ourselves and for others. Only Jesus has your interest at heart, and only men burning with the heartbeat of Jesus Christ, can have your good interest at heart. The second half of the last sentence does imply that we're to be people burning with the heartbeat of Jesus Christ, and who have the interests of other people at heart, unlike Pharaoh.

The devil will go to all lengths to cripple the church with every available weapon, and we've got to match him through God's wisdom, knowledge and resources at our disposal. It is always Satan's intention to entrench slavery and to keep us in spiritual, mental, emotional and material bondage. Perhaps, the most potent of these tricks is ignorance of the truth, which is why God said through His prophet, Amos that "his people perished for lack of knowledge". We've got to resist him and he will flee. The weapons of our warfare are mighty through God to the pulling down of strongholds which the devil seeks to build in our minds and in our Christian experience.

As noted by Nelson Mandela, we cannot effectively preach a message of freedom when we ourselves accept and remain in bondage. You are to stand firm in the liberty Christ has secured for you, and do not be subject to a yoke of slavery of dead religion and traditions of men. It's also easy to backslide, slowly becoming cold hearted, treating sin lightly and walking in dark places, without any meaningful relationship with Jesus the light of the world. When is the church ever going to believe and start to live out what God says we can be? When are we going to believe we can do the things the bible says we can do? We can be free from oppression, because Jesus Christ paid the price, we need to believe it and walk in this promise of freedom.

Action points

If Jesus is not your personal saviour, accept the salvation He freely gives you by believing in Him. Jesus opened the door for both Jew and Gentile, slave and free, rich and poor, male and female to receive the kingdom. Like all presidential pardons, you have to act on this promise. He invites you to repent of sin and to receive his offer of grace and deliverance from all that restricts you. If you are here just exploring Christianity, I congratulate you and hope you will come to the place of accepting the good news which is this: "God loves me, I am a sinner, Christ died for me, if I believe and accept it, I am saved. Just repent and believe and you will be set on the road to an eternal destiny. All other means is an effort in futility".

For us believers, Luke 7:20 and Matthew 11:5 show that the gospel is both to be seen and heard. It's easy to make it only about proclaiming without demonstrating it. Jesus said, go tell John what you **see** and **hear** (Luke 7:20-23) or **hear** and **see** (Matthew 11:5). If people cannot see this good news in action with the captives set free, the sick healed, the bound delivered, material poor supported, it is only half the good news.

Finally, there are others living in darkness and bondage who need freedom. God wants to use you to set free those who have come to accept bondage and darkness as normal. People are wounded and bound in the prison of bitterness and unforgiveness. Paul and Silas did not run away after being freed and God used them to prevent a man from committing suicide and ultimately brought salvation to him and his whole family. Will you step up?

Prologue

Before we finish, let's recap briefly what we started with about the freedom bargains with the question; 'where do you stand among the above 6 C's of Counterfeit, Compromise, Community, Commitment, Cash and Completeness? In the name of Jesus, Christ, I pray that your soul will escape out of the snares and tricks of the enemy. For the snare is broken and we are escaped, our help is in the name of the Lord. I'll like to finish off this book with a quote from one of America's forefathers:

"Is life so dear or peace so sweet as to be purchased at the price of chains and slavery? Forbid it Almighty God! I know not what course others may take but as for me, give me liberty or give me death".[12]

That sounds like Moses challenging God not to undo the great miracle of deliverance he demonstrated when He delivered them from the chains of Egypt, by destroying them for their grave disobedience. That is the language of a man who knows and understands the value, meaning and purpose of freedom and the need to walk continuously in it. I hope and pray, this will be our mind set and experience, in the name of Jesus Christ, who redeemed us with His own blood and seated us in heavenly places, far above all principalities and powers and dominions that seek to hold us in bondage. Be free!

An important decision

I hope you have enjoyed reading this book but I will have failed if I did not provide you an opportunity to respond in the most eternally relevant way. Only people who acknowledge their need of freedom from sin, oppression, failures and weariness are humble enough to receive total freedom. However, only those who repent of their sin and return to God will receive this kingdom. There is a vacuum in the heart of every human being and it's in the shape of Jesus Christ. If life is not making any sense to you, I can say confidently that He is the missing piece of the jigsaw puzzle. Only He can bring meaning to this life and also give you an expectation of eternal life. Please accept Him as your Lord and personal saviour and believe in your heart that God raised Him from the dead for your redemption and total freedom. If the Son (Jesus Christ) sets you free, then you will be free indeed.

If you have been a born again believer but have somehow drifted off as the children of Israel were prone to doing, then make an about turn right now, like the prodigal son and let God the father restore you to a meaningful relationship with Him. Please do it now and contact me on the email address provided at the end of this book and I am sure God will richly bless you.

Bibliography

1. http://www.woodburnmc.org/blog.php?a=following-from-a-distance – (*Accessed 30 March 2013*)
2. Myles Munroe, The Burden of Freedom, Charisma House, Florida, USA (July 2014).
3. http://www.outreachmagazine.com/people/5766-samuel-rodriguez-the-message-and-the-march.html?p=4 (Date accessed 25 April 2014)
4. Obtained from Pastor Steven J Cole's bible study series on James Chapter 2, May 2013. Lesson 8: Why Partiality is Wrong, Part 1 (James 2:1-7). Accessed from https://bible.org/seriespage/lesson-8-why-partiality-wrong-part-1-james-21-7 . Accessed on 25 May 2015.
5. Our Daily Bread, Daily devotion for February 1979.
6. Christian Books online 48. Dwelling Together in Unity http://www.christadelphianbooks.org/booker/bible_fellowship/ch51.html
7. Matthew Henry's Commentary of the Bible.
8. Caleb Ayiku on his Facebook post of 25 May 2015, in celebration of African Union (AU) Day.
9. 7 September 2014, as part of the popular Bible in One Year (BIOY), Nicky Gumbel, Vicar of Holy Trinity Brompton.
10. (http://www.irs.gov/pub/irs-pdf/p1828.pdf - accessed 13 December 2014)
11. Ruth Graham. In Every Pew Sits a Broken Heart: Hope for the Hurting Paperback – 19 Sep 2008.
12. Patrick Henry Speaking at the Virginia Convention, March 23, 1775). Sourced from Leonard Ravenhill's 'Why Revival Tarries, 1972'.

ABOUT THE AUTHOR

Rev Dr Joshua Boateng has been in active Christian ministry for over twenty seven years and is an ordained minister in the body of Christ. He is a Pharmacist by training and Associate Professor (Reader) and Researcher in Pharmaceutical Sciences, which is his other life passion. Joshua is married to Emelia and have three children, named Princella, Leroy and Jason. They reside in Kent, which is in the South Eastern part of England in the United Kingdom.